THE COMPLETE POETRY OF JACK LONDON

Edited by

Daniel J. Wichlan

SECOND EDITION

Little Red Tree Publishing, LLC,
New London, CT. 06320

DEDICATION

In memory of James E. Sisson

Jack London (1876-1916),
while writing *The Sea-Wolf* at
Wake Robin Lodge, Glen Ellen,
California., in 1905.

Copyright © 2014 Daniel J. Wichlan

All rights are reserved under International and Pan-American Copyright Conventions. Except for brief passages quoted in a newspaper, magazine, radio or television review, no part of this book may be reproduced in any form or by any means, electronic or mechanical, including photocopying and recording, or by any information storage and retrieval system, without permission in writing from the publisher.

First Edition 2007
Second Edition 2014

Also available in:

Hardback: 978-1-935656-29-6
Ebook: 978-1-935656-30-2

Cover and Book Design: Michael John Linnard, MCSD
Book set in: Arial, Times New Roman, Trajan Pro

Front cover photograph: This photograph is on permanent display at the Courtesy Special Collections (on-line), Utah State University, Merrill-Cazier Library, and is reprinted by kind permission. The photograph was found loose in Jack London's book *The Sea-Wolf* and inscribed to Charmian London when it was deposited with the book. The photograph is of Jack London while writing "The Sea-Wolf" at Wake Robin Lodge, Glen Ellen, California, 1905 and was probably taken by Charmian London.

Back cover photograph: This photograph is used with the kind permission of the The Huntington Library. The photograph of London is cropped from a much larger photograph showing a group of four (left to right) include: George Sterling, James (Jimmy) Hopper, Harry Leon Wilson and Jack London.

All photographs distributed throughout this book are in the public domain. The majority collected from the Huntington Library, or Utah State University, Merrill-Crazier Library.

Library of Congress Cataloging-in-Publication Data

London, Jack, 1876-1916.
 [Poems]
 The complete poetry of Jack London / edited by Daniel J. Wichlan. -- 2nd ed.
   p. cm.
 Includes bibliographical references and index.
 ISBN 978-1-935656-28-9 (pbk. : alk. paper)
 I. Wichlan, Daniel J. II. Title.
 PS3523.O46A6 2014
 818'.5209--dc22
                    2014050901

Little Red Tree Publishing, LLC,
635 Ocean Avenue,
New London, CT 06320.
website: www.littleredtree.com

ACKNOWLEDGEMENT

It is most appropriate to begin by acknowledging James E. Sisson to whom this book is dedicated. It was his pioneering research of Jack London's poetry that both inspired and enabled this book.

It is also appropriate to acknowledge Michael Linnard who conceived this project and who influenced its scope to its present form despite the protestations of myself and whose knowledge of and comprehensive research on the authorship of the poetry used throughout the writings of Jack London was invaluable. Credit is also due to Michael for his diligent research and creation of Appendix A.

Next it follows that I acknowledge David Hartzell, webmaster of "The World of Jack London," who allowed me to post London's poetry on his website, which event led to my connection with Michael.

Finally, I cannot fail to acknowledge my wife, Barbara Wichlan, whose untiring and unerring proof reading yielded pristine copy for your perusal.

CONTENTS

Foreword by Michael Linnard   viii
Preface to Second Edition by Daniel J Wichlan   x
Preface by Daniel J Wichlan   xii
Introduction (Revised) by Daniel J. Wichlan   xv

Section A: Jack London's Published Poetry

1	Effusion	2
2	The Mammon Worshippers	3
3	Daybreak	4
4	The Worker and the Tramp	5
5	Lovers Liturgy	6
6	He Chortled With Glee	8
7	When He Came In	9
8	If I Were God	10
9	The Way of War	11
10	Sonnet	13
11	Sea Sprite and the Shooting Star	14
12	In a Year	17
13	A Passionate Author to His Love	18
14	Abalone Song	19
15	Of Man of the Future	21
16	On the Face of the Earth You Are the One	22
17	Tick! Tick! Tick!	23
18	Oh You Everybody's Girl	25

Section B: Jack London's Unpublished Poetry

19	Gold	28
20	Je Vis En Espoir	30
21	My Confession	31
22	The Socialist Dream	32
23	Hors De Saison	35
24	He Never Tried Again	37
25	The Klondyker's Dream	38
26	Moods	40
27	Cupid's Deal	41
28	Republican Battle-Hymn	43
29	Republican Rallying Song	45
30	My Little Palmist	46
31	Ballade of the False Lover	48
32	Return of Ulysses—A Modern Version	49
33	Rainbows End	55
34	His Trip to Hades	56
35	A Heart	57
36	The Song of the Flames	60
37	The Gift of God	61

38	Memory	63
39	George Sterling	64
40	Homeland	65
41	And Some Night	66
42	Your Kiss	67
43	Too Late	68
44	When All the World Shouted My Name	69

Section C: **Poetry in Jack London's Writing Attributed to Others** — 73

Section D: **Poetry in Jack London's Writing Unattributed to Others** — 123

Section E: **Play—Attributed to Jack London**

The Acorn Planter	132

Section F: **Play—Attributed to George Sterling**

The First Poet	184

Section G: **Jack London's—Book Inscriptions:**

Charmian Kittredge-London	198
Bessie Maddern, Joan and Becky London	212

Appendix A:
Jack London: No 1—Magazine Sales—1898 to May 1900 — 219

Appendix B:
Jack London: A Chronological Biography — 227

Appendix C:
Jack London: Published Books—First Editions — 231

Index of Poem Titles and First Verses	233
Index Poets and Authors	236
Bibliography of Jack London's Poetry	239
About the Author—Daniel J. Wichlan	242

FOREWORD

It is a without question a privilege for Little Red Tree Publishing, LLC, of New London, Connecticut, to be offered the opportunity to publish *The Complete Poetry of Jack London* edited by Daniel J. Wichlan.

A book of new information, insight and actual discovery about an icon of American and World literature would at first glance seem unlikely or even implausible given the length of time that has elapsed since his untimely death almost 98 years ago at the age of 40. However, due to more than 20 years of meticulous research in numerous archives and databases by Daniel, previously unpublished work of Jack London will be published in this book for the first time.

For those who might be curious to know the background as to how this book came to be conceived and produced I think a few words of explanation may be required. In fact the origins of this book are as interesting, bizarre and unconnected as they are a product of painstaking research and an undying passion by a researcher of legendary status, within the London community, combined with an appropriate quantity of fate and good fortune.

Essentially as a consequence of a chance meeting in Louisiana on a typically sultry and balmy spring evening, in early 2007, and a lively conversation with a crusty old country and western songwriter I was acutely embarrassed at my scant knowledge of Jack London and his work. Under pointed questioning and accusatory eyes I struggled to find any evidence in my memory of London's work outside of a brief mention by one of my literary heroes George Orwell. I vaguely recalled to mind that Orwell (Eric Blair) cited London's book *The People of the Abyss* as one of the most influential books he had ever read and the inspiration not only to become a writer but to literally follow in his footsteps writing his own work *Down and Out in Paris and London*. Later he went on to write the classic *Animal Farm* and *1984*. My limp response was summarily dismissed as derisory and woefully inadequate from someone purporting to be a "publisher."

Suitably chastened by this somewhat uncompromisingly brutal encounter I took the next opportunity to investigate and research the life and work of Jack London. I was amazed to encounter a monumental amount of information online and subsequently spent countless hours reading about the life and work of this remarkable American writer. I was immediately drawn into the world of a man who blazed a trail of creativity, rarely equalled, and in the process produced a simply staggering amount of published work within a short period of time of less than twenty years.

In the course of this wonderful journey of discovery about Jack London I noticed an item regarding previously published and unpublished poetry of Jack London compiled by Daniel J. Wichlan on "The World of Jack London" website. Undoubtedly like most people unfamiliar with the vast range of Jack London's writing I was drawn to reading further. Nearing the end of a fascinating piece of writing describing his research into the poetry of Jack London I came across a statement about how Daniel had been unable to find a suitable publisher for his book. In fact as a direct consequence of the dearth of publishers the article I was reading would not have existed at all.

This immediately set my mind into shock mode: to think that any publisher, anywhere in the world, would not wish to publish a book about Jack London seemed suddenly incomprehensible if not unbelievable. Subsequently I made contact with Daniel and offered to publish the book immediately. It must be said clearly that the present scope of this book far exceeds its original intent and stems from numerous discussions about the implications of the title and how best to establish and present poetry as the driving force behind the literary work of Jack London. Generally speaking a title such as this book would normally be reserved for a poet with a considerable body of work but I contend that in the case of Jack London it is fully warranted and justified.

It is our firm belief that a full exploration of the verse to be found in all aspects of the published and unpublished writing of Jack London is long over due as the true genesis of his literary style. This book will at last reveal and establish the fact that Jack London was essentially a poet who wrote fiction and nonfiction rather than a writer of fiction and nonfiction who also wrote poetry.

Even the most cursory examination of his life will reveal the fact that he assiduously studied, read, wrote and discussed poetry constantly throughout his life and infused his writing with poetry whenever the opportunity arose. Simply put, poetry was his life. Therefore, we present this book, edited by Daniel J. Wichlan, as the definitive complete poetry of Jack London

Michael Linnard, CEO
Little Red Tree Publishing, LLC
New London, CT 2007

PREFACE TO THE SECOND EDITION

The editor and his publisher are encouraged by the response to the first edition of this book to the point that we have embarked on this second edition. The chief differences offered by this edition are corrections, of course, and, more significantly, the findings of further research including the addition of one very significant poem—"The Passionate Author to His Love"—which is a love poem that London wrote to Anna Strunsky. Also noteworthy is the attribution of much of the previously unattributed poetry used by London in his writing. This is the result of much diligent research by my publisher.

Whenever one claims to have collected the complete works of a writer, one is subject to being proven wrong by later research especially when dealing with as prolific a writer as Jack London who was also published internationally and, in this case, under a pseudonym. Once again we make the claim in this edition that it represents the complete poetry of London, i.e., as complete as any good faith effort can be expected to achieve. Having said this, we know from London's letters and writing log notes that there are "lost poems," some of which are identified at the beginning of the "Unpublished Poetry" section of the book. It is entirely possible that somewhere, sometime these may be found.

The response to the first edition also gave me a new knowledge of book reviewers from the author's point of view. I now divide them into three groups: first, those who are good at what they do and who understand the intent of the book and who objectively comment on how well or poorly that intent was executed; second, those who are more interested in demonstrating their own knowledge of the subject matter and who dote on their own clever writing; and, third, those who request review copies of the book but who don't bother to write reviews. I will say no more about this third group.

The second group, however, is worth further comment and actually inspired some changes to the Introduction of this edition. The thesis of the book is that the significance of London's poetry and his love of poetry is not the poetry itself but rather how it influenced his writing and how it energized his creativity. Enough of the first group of reviewers got this point such that I don't believe that the failure of the second group to do so was due to my shortcomings in expressing it. Either it was too subtle for them or they didn't read the entire Introduction. Therefore, this thesis is stated as clearly and as simply as possible in the first two paragraphs of the new Introduction and further developed later in the original portion of the Introduction. Too many of this second group focused too much on the archaic style of London's poetry and one of them actually condemned the title, *The Complete Poetry of Jack London,* because it included not only his poetry but also his use of the poetry of others.

However, as an author or editor, it is probably better to be misunderstood or abused than it is to be ignored. It is this broad and varied response to the first edition that has inspired the author and his publisher to try to do better in this second edition.

Daniel J. Wichlan
San Francisco, 2014

Jack London in Boston 1906

PREFACE

My awareness of and interest in Jack London began on my tenth birthday when my father gave me a collection of London's short stories. I vividly recall staying up all night and reading the book from cover to cover. As a result I became an avid reader and a devotee of Jack London. I soon became a passionate reader of London's fiction which I quickly exhausted. Later, as a young adult, I reread the fiction and then moved on to the nonfiction. Next I began to read all of the biographical and critical writing pertaining to London that I could find. By this time, my passion had become an obsession, and I set out on a mission to acquire and read every word that London ever wrote for publication. Effectively this goal excluded only personal letters, many of which I have also read.

My goal drove me to find rare uncollected articles and search various archives, both foreign and domestic, for uncompleted and unpublished works. I spent much of my discretionary time over the last two decades in this search. Most of what I found falls into the nonfiction category which I have published separately. However, I was pleasantly surprised to find a significant body of poetry. As I read London's poetry, I began to acquire a new insight into his writing. I went back to the biographical writings, letters and some miscellaneous works that I recalled mentioning London's interest in poetry. Once I collected and organized these, I gained an entirely new understanding of London as a writer. Jack London was essentially a poet who, unable to earn a living as such, wrote fiction and nonfiction to make a living and to finance his continuing interest in poetry. Proof of this bold statement lies in the documents presented in this book and in the lyrical writing and frequent poetic quotations throughout London's books.

Today, any interest in London's poetry is overshadowed to the point of obscurity by his fiction and nonfiction such that my search for a publisher for the poetry was fruitless and frustrating. Out of frustration, and in an attempt to share what I had found with the London community, I posted some of the poetry in this book on "The World of Jack London" website. This posting proved to be most fortuitous because it brought London's poetry to the attention of Michael Linnard, the CEO of Little Red Tree Publishing in New London, Connecticut. Michael is himself a poet, and he immediately saw the potential in publishing London's poetry. In fact, his vision went far beyond what I had posted on the website and created this book whose scope I will now describe.

This book is about Jack London's profound love of poetry and how it influenced his writing. Its scope includes not only the poetry that London wrote but also the poetry of others that he so frequently and effectively embedded in his work. This book, for the first time, presents a collection of all the verse used in London's writing and identifies which were written by London and which were written by other poets. The book reprints eighteen of his separately published poems (Section A), and also for the first time publishes twenty-six of his poems (Section B).

His entire body of writing was independently reviewed twice to identify any verse that it contained and, although this author and his publisher cannot guarantee inclusion of 100% of that verse, due to human error, we are confident that we are close to 100% and that any omissions are insignificant. After extracting the verse throughout London's work, it was necessary to search for the author's identity since London frequently embedded the verse unattributed in his writing. This is presented in (Section C) "Poetry in London's Writing Attributed to Others." What remained after this search appears in the section "Poetry in London's Writing Unattributed to Others," (Section D). The content of this section was probably written by London. Also included are two stage plays in verse that London published in the last year of his life (Sections E and F) that mark a return to poetry he predicted many years earlier.

In the interest of comprehensiveness, we have also included the inscriptions that London wrote in copies of the first editions of his books to his second wife Charmian (Mate-Woman) which are poetic in nature. Also included are the inscriptions to his first wife, Bessie Maddern, (Mother-Girl) and his daughters Joan and Bess. These are in a section so entitled (Section G).

This book was inspired by James E. Sisson, to whom I have dedicated this book, and who was working on his version of *The Complete Poetry of Jack London* as far back as 1970. The July 1970 issue of "The London Collector" (a self-styled "fanzine" or amateur literary magazine dedicated to Jack London) featured a preview of Sisson's manuscript. It was to include thirty-two poems, nineteen of which were unpublished at the time. In so far as I can determine, Sisson's book was not published. Nonetheless, the author is indebted to the pioneering research that Sisson conducted with respect to Jack London's poetry.

As described above, the scope of the present book greatly exceeds that of Sisson's proposal by including more published and unpublished poetry (forty-four versus thirty-two); London's use of possibly his own unattributed poetry and the poetry of others in his prose works; stage plays in verse; and book inscriptions. Therefore, to call this book "the complete poetry" is a reasonable claim. There are doubtlessly numerous poetic inscriptions by London made in books still in private hands (He probably inscribed hundreds, if not thousands, of copies). He also wrote thousands of letters, many of which remain in private collections, and some of which likely contain poetic fragments, if not whole verses. These inscriptions and letters can never be collected in their entirety. What this book presents, for the first time, is the complete poetry written for publication of one of America's most famous and celebrated writers, with the exception of the inscriptions to his family. This, the author believes, is a significant and justifiable exception.

The book is organized chronologically within each section by date published or date written, if previously unpublished. The original punctuation and spelling have been preserved. Likewise London's use of the word "verse" to refer to a single line of poetry has been preserved throughout the text. At the back of this book we have added, for the interest and convenience of both researchers and new readers unfamiliar with the full extent of Jack London's work: twenty-eight reproduced pages of London's poetic notes and studies in poetry; a brief chronological biography of Jack London, including all his books in the year they were published; a list of all Jack London's first edition books; an index of the titles and first verses of London's poems; an index of poets and authors referred to in this book and finally a full bibliography of his poetry.

Daniel J. Wichlan
San Francisco, 2007

INTRODUCTION

(Revised from the original 2007 edition)

Jack London's love of poetry was the genesis of his literary artistry. His passion for poetry was born at the age of ten when Ina Coolbrith, who later became the first poet laureate of California, began mentoring him at the Oakland Free Public Library where she was the librarian. Her influence on London continued until his death in 1916 when he published *The Acorn Planter*, a play in verse. London later referred to Coolbrith as his "literary mother." As a result of this relationship, London developed into a much different writer than he otherwise might have been.

It is not the quality of London's poetry that justifies this collection, but rather it is the insight that it provides to his writing creativity. When judged by modern standards, London's poetry does not stand out, although its classical style and structure do show good writing discipline and craftsmanship that carried over to his prose work.

Jack London had the heart and soul of a poet as demonstrated by his love of and passion for poetry that are documented in this book. Few prose writers exceed his knowledge and understanding of writing poetry and the breadth of his reading of poetry was phenomenal. London used poetry, his and others, extensively throughout his writing, in fact, thirty-two of his fifty-five books (see Appendix C) contain significant amounts of poetry.

But London was much more than an aspiring poet. He was one of the greatest short story writers in the English language. He helped to mold that genre into its present day form through his strong characterization, his realistic style of writing and his power of vivid description. He was also the best selling American novelist of the first two decades of the Twentieth Century. Consequently, whatever London wrote, including his poetry, remains of interest today. In fact, with this second edition of his poetry, fifty-three of his fifty-five books remain in print a century after their original publication.

London owes much of his success to the richness of language and emotionally stirring descriptions used throughout his writing. This language and these descriptions frequently reached lyrical levels as in his masterpiece *The Call of the Wild* and its companion book, *White Fang*. London's poetic instinct is the origin of his writing prowess and reading and understanding his poetry is essential to reading and understanding his fiction.

On page 220 of *John Barleycorn*, his autobiographical novel, London tells us that in early 1897, after dropping out of the University of California, he,

> "...decided immediately to embark on my career. I had four preferences: first, music; second, poetry; third, the writing of philosophic, economic, and political essays; and, fourth, and last, and least, fiction writing. I resolutely cut out music as impossible, settled down in my bedroom, and tackled my second, third and fourth choices simultaneously... I wrote... humorous verse, verse of all sorts from triolets and sonnets to blank verse tragedy and elephantine epics in Spenserian stanzas. On occasion I composed steadily, day after day, for fifteen hours a day. At times I forgot to eat, or refused to tear myself away from my passionate outpouring in order to eat."

London wrote the preceding in 1913 wherein he claimed to be a poet first and foremost. This claim is supported by his log of "Magazine Sales" that he began keeping in 1898 and which kept track of his manuscript submissions and publications. The first 28 pages (reproduced in Appendix A) of this log constitute a primer on writing poetry that London compiled for his own use. In it he defines the various poetic structures and offers examples of each. He also describes a variety of meters and illustrates each. He quotes verse from some of his favorite poets (Dryden, Pope, Shakespeare, Shelley, Burns and Tennyson) and scans this verse so as to identify the meter used. The 1893 book, *Orthometry: A Treatise on The Art of Versification and the Technicalities of Poetry* by Robert F. Brewer, is a handbook for poets and it appears to have been a primary source for London's study of poetry. London's manuscript log represents his "diary" as a professional writer, and it is clear that he embarked on his writing career with the intent of becoming, above all else, a published poet.

The intensity of his poetic writing, as described in *John Barleycorn*, strongly suggests that London's total poetic production exceeded the 44 that are listed in the "Jack London's Published Poetry" and "Jack London's Unpublished Poetry," sections (A and B) of this book. If all of the poems in the "Poetry in London's Writing Unattributed to Others," section (D) of this book are attributed to him, it would increase his known poetic production to 61 poems and songs, including the five known lost poems.

This latter premise would seem to be a reasonable one. London clearly did not totally discard the unpublished poetry that he had written during the 1897 to 1899 period. For example, "Effusion" was written in May 1897, and London used it in his *Human Drift* essay that was published in January 1911. He likely did this in other cases such as those listed in the "London's Writing Unattributed to Others" (section D) of this book.

The other noteworthy point that London makes in the preceding statement from *John Barleycorn* is that music was his first choice in writing and poetry was his second choice. This predilection is reinforced in a January 8, 1905 interview in the *Oakland Enquirer* in which London says that the success of "'Call of Wild' draws him to poetry and song." He talks about his passion for poetry and song and how his use of language and descriptions in his masterpiece, *The Call of the Wild*, are influenced by this passion. He goes on to say that he hopes that the success of this book will enable him to devote more time to poetry and song writing. His proclivity for poetry and song is also evident in his 1906 parallel novel, *White Fang*, in which there is even more lyricism.

Consider this passage from chapter III of *The Call of the Wild*,

> "With the aurora borealis flaming coldly overhead, or the stars leaping in the frost dance, and the land numb and frozen under its pall of snow, this song of the huskies might have been the defiance of life, only it was pitched in minor key, with long-drawn wailings and half-sobs, and was more the pleading of life, the articulate travail of existence. It was an old song, old as the breed itself—one of the first songs of the younger world in a day when songs were sad. It was invested with the woe of unnumbered generations, this plaint by which Buck was so strangely stirred. When he moaned and sobbed, it was with the pain of living that was of old the pain of his wild fathers, and the fear and mystery of the cold and dark that was to them fear and mystery. And that he should be stirred by it marked the completeness with which he harked back through the ages of fire and roof to the raw beginnings of life in the howling ages."

Also consider this passage from chapter V,

> "It was beautiful spring weather, but neither dogs nor humans were aware of it. Each day the sun rose earlier and set later. It was dawn by three in the morning, and twilight lingered till nine at night. The whole long day was a blaze of sunshine. The ghostly winter silence had given way to the great spring murmur of awakening life. This murmur arose from all the land, fraught with the joy of living. It came from the things that lived and moved again, things which had been as dead and which had not moved during the long months of frost. The sap was rising in the pines. The willows and aspens were bursting out in young buds. Shrubs and vines were putting on fresh garbs of green. Crickets sang in the nights, and in the days all manner of creeping, crawling things rustled forth into the sun. Partridges and woodpeckers were booming and knocking in the forest. Squirrels were chattering, birds singing, and overhead honked the wild-fowl driving up from the south in cunning wedges that split the air."

London began in *White Fang* where he had left off in *The Call of the Wild*. Consider the opening paragraph from *White Fang*,

> "Dark spruce forest frowned on either side the frozen waterway. The trees had been stripped by a recent wind of their white covering of frost, and they seemed to lean towards each other, black and ominous, in the fading light. A vast silence reigned over the land. The land itself was a desolation, lifeless, without movement, so lone and cold that the spirit of it was not even that of sadness. There was a hint in it of laughter, but of a laughter more terrible than any sadness—a laughter that was mirthless as the smile of the Sphinx, a laughter cold as the frost and partaking of the grimness of infallibility. It was the masterful and incommunicable wisdom of eternity laughing at the futility of life and the effort of life. It was the Wild, the savage, frozen-hearted Northland Wild."

Poetry and song seem to be intertwined in the London psyche. Indeed, the lyrics and rhythm of song are closely akin to the words and meter of poetry. Therefore, this book includes London's writing and use of both; although poetry is sometimes used in the generic sense to mean both.

This relationship between poetry and song and London's approach to interpreting and writing poetry are elucidated in this September 15, 1898 letter to Edward Applegarth who was an aspiring poet. In this lengthy letter, London both critiques Applegarth's poetry and delivers the equivalent of a short dissertation on writing poetry. It illustrates London's deep technical knowledge of writing poetry,

> "In poetry, as everything else, results are judged, rather than legitimacy. Our best writers are full of technical errors. If you can bend the technique to the sense, the former not being glaring & the latter the real thought & utterance of poetry, I am sure it is pardonable. Scan the blank verse of some of the strongest of Shakespear *(sic)* & you will find that I am right. Poetry in the English language is bound to always be stilted, but the true aim of the artist should be, or the very essence of the art is to reduce the stilt to minimum & still musically voice the poetic thought or fancy. Take Longfellow's 'Psalm of Life' break up the stanzas & let line, or rather, verse follow verse, in prose style retaining same punctuation, and what do you find? That thought follows on thought, clause follows clause & sentence follows sentence so that if you for the moment could eliminate your consciousness of metre & rhyme, you would remark what a perfect prose style it was.
>
> As against it array this verse from Browning:
>
> > 'So I said & did
> > Simply. As simply followed, not at first
> > But with the outbreak of misfortune, still
> > One comment on the saying & doing—what?
> > No blush at the avowal you dared buy
> > A girl of age beseems your grand daughter,
> > Like ox or ass?'
> > — *The Ring & the Book.*

I like your poems, and as I am replying at once, have not had time to choose my favorite. One thing you have got, and you have it good—it is the very essence & the fundament principle of poetry; it is real poetical thought & fancy. Without it, there can be no poetry, though miles & miles of perfect, musical metre & ryhme be written. Turn to Chaucer's *Canterbury Tales*. Open at the poet's tale. It is a bit against the French style existing at that time; which consisted of beautiful verse most remarkable for both its beauty & absence of thought. The poet goes on & on but what does he tell? Nothing, absolutely nothing. You will notice that the audience grows impatient & the poet is finally forced to tell his tale in prose, the only prose tale in the whole collection.

I like your preferred ending in 'The Law of Actions,' better.

Outside of that let me scan your double set of 2nd & 3rd stanzas on the following page showing imperfect & halting meter. (By the way, you call a stanza a verse—remember that a verse is a line.)

With all force as ye could see	1. With all force as ye could see
(If ye fairly sought it),	2. ....
That ef/fects must/follow/cause	3. Cause &/effect/must ev/er be/
(But perhaps ye thought it)	4. ....
Follow/always/the same/way	5. Follow/ing in/the self/same way
For they cannot go astray.	6. For they cannot go astray.
With all mind, as ye shall know	7. With all mind as ye shall know
....	....
Mind effects must follow cause	9. Mind ef/fects af/ter cause/must go
....	....
Follow as night the day	....
And they cannot go astray	....
	(Don't mind pencil scanning)

Scan the two third lines: -^/-^/-^/— and -^/^-/^-/^-/. Fifth lines & ninth lines you will notice have similar error on scanning. All you have to do is to repeat first one line & then the other to notice the tremendous difference. You may have thought that you were writing this in Iambic but it is really trochaic. I mistook it at first. The preferred stanza is the perfect stanza. The 1, 3, 5 & 6 verses of preferred stanza are Trunctated Trochaic Tetrameter.

Trunctated means that the final unaccented syllable is cut off, thus:

    ′   ′   ′   ′
    That ef/fects must/follow/cause—/

The trouble in writing this is that in the middle of the verse you are liable to jump the meter & go over to Iambic.

You will notice that the 2 & 4 verses are perfect Trochaic trimeter, thus

    ′   ′   ′
    If ye/fairly/sought it/

The combinations of trunctated Trochaic Tetrameter verses with perfect Trochaic trimeter, make beautiful poetry.

You will also notice that in the third, fifth & ninth verses of unpreferred Stanzas, that in scanning no elision is possible for making the meter ring true.

Take the next to last verse in 'Problem of Evil': On the rock of evoloution *(sic)*. There is no verse like it in the whole poem.

It breaks the unity of meter & is a positive discord, a discord coming above all at the very last when the final taste is being left in our mouth, and said taste must be good. You know the effect of anti-climax in style; this has the same effect only more so.

I like the ring of your verse: 'Above all, below all, & in all.' Never sacrifice thought to sound, ryhme or meter. If you cannot clothe the thought without injuring it—throw it away.

In the first verse of 'A Question' you have the word 'blinking.' To make this ryhme you prostitute the thought & the sound. There is no real poetical delicacy in the sound or the thought of 'blinking.'

Take for instance, 'grinding'—in the description of a May morning or a lover's song, it would have no poetic sound, it would be a discord. Yet use it in describing a great disaster or battle & you will see at once, *by its sound*, describes the things & the feelings that they cause.

Take Tennyson's 'Bugle Song' for an illustration of imitative sound. Feel the *hush* that breathes forth from

> 'The splendor falls on castle walls
> And snowy summits old in story.'

And the *pure* tone, *so thin & clear* of

> 'O hark, O hear! how thin & clear,
>   And thinner, clearer, farther going,
> O sweet & far, from cliff & scar,
>   The horns of Elfland faintly blowing.'

And the full, deep feeling from

> 'O love, they die in yon rich sky,
>   They faint on hill or field or river;
> *Our* echoes *roll from soul to soul,*
>   And *grow forever and forever.*
>
> As the sea shell's song seems ever
> A sad echo of the sea.'

This is simply magnificent—a delicate fancy, perfectly & most delicately clothed.

But in same poem your 'sad sad' and 'solemn solemn' constitutes one of the worst conditions of *pleonasm* or *Superfluity*, that of *repetition*. Now *repetition* is sometimes most necessary & most powerful, but you must exercise your discretion & *taste*. As you know, taste is a most *important* attribute to true *poesy*.

Look up the use of *alliteration* and *assonance*—great factors for *putting* music, over & above meter & ryhme, into poetry.

In your line 'Above all, below all & in all' you will notice the full, round sound called the *orotund*, expressive of deep feeling, a sort of soul reaching sound. Compare with 'Our echoes roll from soul to soul'.

In 'To the Children' capitalize 'might have been' Might have been. It is proper, it diversifies the mere look of the verse, and is significant & impressive.
Your verse breathes a faint perfume as it seems to me of Swineburne, Tennyson & Browning—thought especially in relation to the latter. But I don't know as I have read no poetry for 14 months & am very rusty in all such things. But go ahead old man, you are doing dam well, send us some more.

I must close this letter as I have been writing like a tiger all day, it is now past one in the morning & I must be up at five to go riding with Mabel. Your letter just came & I reply at once.

Previous to my going to the Clondyke, I had just taken up the study of poetry individually. Will send you my every attempt. Since my return I have written just four verses—wrote them this morning as an introduction to the article I am now on—a sort of keynote you know:

> We worshipped at alien altars; we bowed our heads in the dust;
>   Our law was might is the mightiest; our creed was unholy lust;
> Our law & our creed we followed—strange is the tale to tell—
> For our law & our creed we followed into the pit of hell.
>   —*The Mammon Worshippers.*

You will notice the *pleonasm*—I believe that it gives power here—too long to go into discussion however."

London had little commercial success with his poetry, but it represented a deep-rooted passion with him. Between March 1897 and August 1899 London wrote at least 35 poems, but only two of these were published during that time period (another 16 were published later after London was otherwise successful). London apparently did not take this rejection of "his first literary love" lightly. In an 1898 letter, Mable Applegarth, his first romantic love, criticized him for spending so much time writing poetry as opposed to writing stories that he could sell. In his December 6, 1898 response to her London pointed out that the discipline of writing poetry enhanced his ability to write prose. He stated that his poems "were studies in structure and versification" and a "fine drill, forcing one to be trite, to sum his thoughts in a small compass, to condense." Prose and poetry were closely integrated in London's mind.

In a February 3, 1900 letter to Anna Strunsky London articulated what was to become his lifelong dilemma,

> "Poetry? What wouldn't I give to be just able to sit down and write ambitious work? But then it doesn't pay, and I don't. One must try one's hand for so long in order to get the touch, and the many attempts have no market value."

Ten years later he expressed this same point of view in a November 19, 1910 letter to Henry Noyes, another aspiring poet,

> "Nobody makes any money out of poetry in the United States. I may state flatly and absolutely, that to-day in the United States no man writing serious poetry makes the expenses of publication. There are one or two men, such as Wallace Irwin, writing humorous verses and doggerel for the magazines, who make a living and a good living. And that is all.
>
> Here is where I have to bring my practical, experienced judgment to bear, and tell you that there is not one chance in a million for you to make two cents out of your collection of poetry. I have a friend, whom I believe to be the greatest living poet in the United States (George Sterling). He has published three volumes of great poetry. They have never brought him a cent. The average poet of the day who brings out a book of verses, pays for publication of the same in advance, and never gets his money back, is a sweeping statement I am making, and it is a true one."

Despite this pessimism, London did not lose hope of some day turning back to writing poetry. In a February 1900 letter to Anna Strunsky, London wrote,

> "As to the box. Please take good care of the contents. And don't mix them up, please. I haven't written any poetry for months. Those you see are my experiments (studies in structure and meter) and though they be failures I have not surrendered. When I am financially secure, some day, I shall continue with them—unless I have prostituted myself beyond *redemption.*"

Herein London clearly states that he is merely taking respite from poetry with the intention of resuming one day.

By 1906, London's ardor for poetry had cooled. In a letter to author J. Torrey

Connor, London writes,

> "Long years ago, before I sold my first thing to a magazine, I dabbled a little in poetry; and then, resolutely, I cut poetry out. From that day to this, I have never attempted a line of it despite a sneaking belief that I could develop into a pretty good poet. If an editor should appear before me right now, and offer to exchange his birthright for a mess of my poetry, I would tell him nothing doing."

The fact that London wrote poetry so diligently for two and one-half years and then stopped so suddenly and "resolutely" suggests a traumatic event or, at least, a profound discouragement, because we know that London's love of poetry did not cease. London frequently read poetry, his and others, at social gatherings throughout his life.

London's second wife, Charmian, refers to this practice of reading poetry in Volume I of *The Book of Jack London* on page 362,

> "Those Wednesday afternoons and evenings will never fade to the lucky souls privileged to share in them, filled as they were with merriest and noisiest of jollity and sport; card-games—whist, poker, pedro, 'black-jack.' rapid-fire of wits. And there was no lack of music—piano and singing, ringing voices—and poetry. Arthur Symons, Le Gallienne, Swinburne, the Rosettis, Fitzgerald, Bierce, Henley—these and many others were read aloud around the long oaken table, or lolling about the roomy veranda where swung the hammock. Now it would be George Sterling's hushed recitation, or Jack's vibrant tone, or Anna's mellow, golden throat—all the others hanging tremulous on the music of speech from these receptive ones who could not wait to make known their beloved of the poets. Blessing it was to sit under the involuntary young teachers of good and gracious ways of the spirit."

Charmian's claim here is substantiated by the poetry in the "Attributed Poetry" (Section C) of this book, in which all of the above named poets are represented.

On page 369 of Volume II, Charmian continues,

> "Evening after evening he read aloud from Percy's 'Reliques of Ancient English Poetry,' and reread certain of these to Beth and to his two 'saints,' my sister Emma Growall, and my uncle's wife, Villa Wiley. Two large volumes we went through, and the third and last to Page 288. The next selection is 'St. George for England,' and Jack's book-mark, the ubiquitous safety-match, still rests between the leaves. Dryden's 'Jealousie Tyrant of the Mind' was an especial treasure to us. I shall hear until I die Jack's voice of the lover in 'The Nut-Browne Mayd,' which he never tired of repeating, and which I called for over and over, if only for the spell of the 'viols' in his throat, and to see, under the long curl of lashes, the eyes he raised to mine at the verse-ends: 'I love but you alone.'"

London would seem to have sublimated his love for poetry as opposed to abandoning it. And this is the real significance of London's poetry. As a separate entity his poetry is not memorable; however, its underlying creative spirit had a profound effect on his ability to write lyrical prose when needed. As evidenced in the "Attributed Poetry" and "Unattributed Poetry" sections (C and D) of this book, London generously used the poetry of others and possibly his own in his writing of prose. Knowing London's poetry is essential to understanding his development as a writer.

Toward the end of his life, London revived his interest in writing poetry as he had predicted in his February 1900 letter to Anna Strunsky. In 1915 he published the lyrics to three songs that he had written that are included in the "Published Poetry" section (A) of this book. In 1916, the year of his death, he published *The Acorn Planter*, a play in verse, which is included in its entirety in the "Stage Plays" section (E) of this book. Later that year, he published *The Turtles of Tasman* which includes the one act play, "The First Poet," which is also included in the following section (F) of this book. Although this play was actually written by George Sterling, it is included on the same principle as was the other poetry that London "borrowed throughout his writing." London likely related to this play because of the conflict that it portrays between the poet and a society that demands food be put on the table to the exclusion of artistic endeavors.

When thoughtfully considering the foregoing, it is apparent that Jack London was a poet who, out of economic necessity, made his living writing prose. Prose that at times was so lyrical and so full of imagery that it teeters on that invisible pale between prose and poetry. London had the head, heart and soul of a poet; his intellectual, emotional and spiritual essence was poetic, and this essence is the source of the creativity and passion with which he wrote. Had he lived longer, and as he achieved greater financial independence, he doubtlessly would have continued the trend that he established during the last 18 months of his life by writing more poetry and song and moving ever closer to his life-long goal. London wrote to live but he lived to write, read and recite poetry. Everything quoted above from his novels, letters and interviews points to this conclusion. This belief is essential to understanding London as a literary artist and as a man. Test this premise as you read the poetry that follows, whether it be independently presented or embedded in his other writing.

Daniel J. Wichlan
San Francisco, 2014

SECTION A

JACK LONDON'S PUBLISHED POETRY

The poems in this section are presented in the order in which they were written (when known).

Perhaps conspicuous by their absence are the poems:

> "The Lazy Man's Prayer"
> "The Scissorbill's Prayer" or "Morning Prayer"
> "On the Face of the Earth"
> "Sweeney's"
> "Yukon Belle"
> "Belle of the Yukon"

These poems have been mistakenly attributed to London in various articles and biographies such as Irving Stone's *Sailor on Horseback*, but there is no documentation in any of the London collections to support these undocumented claims. In fact, Stone's "biography" is notorious for its erroneous claims. Later editions were retitled as "a biographical novel."

EFFUSION

Thou canst not weep;
Nor ask I for a year
To rid me of my woes
Or make my life more dear.

The mystic chains that bound
Thy all-fond heart to mine,
Alas! asundered are
For now and for all time.

In vain you strove to hide,
From vulgar gaze of man,
The burning glance of love
That none but Love can scan.

Go on thy starlit way
And leave me to my fate;
Our souls must needs unite—
But, God! 'twill be too late.

Written in May 1897.

This poem was first published in the essay "The Human Drift" in the January 1911 issue of *The Forum*. The poem was later collected in *The Human Drift* as the title story in February 1917.

THE MAMMON WORSHIPPERS

We worshipped at alien altars; we bowed our heads in the dust;
Our Law was might is the mightiest; our Creed was unholy lust;
Our Law and our Creed we followed—strange is the tale to tell—
For our Law and our Creed we followed into the pit of hell.

Written in May 1897.

This poem was first published in *The Saturday Evening Post* on December 25, 1976. The poem also appears in the story "The Devil's Dice Box."

DAYBREAK

The blushing dawn the easy illumes,
The birds their merry matins sing,
The buds breath forth their sweet perfumes,
And butterflies are on the wing.

I pause beneath the window high,
The door is locked, the house is quiet;
'Tis there, abed, she sure must lie,—
To Wake her,—ah! I'll try it.

And pebbles hurtling through the air,
Strike full upon the window-pane,
Awakening her who slumbers there
With their insistent hurricane.

Ye gods! in my imagination,
The wondrous scene do I behold—
A nymph's bewildered consternation
At summons thus so fierce and bold.

A moment passes, then I see
The gauzy curtains drawn aside,
And sweet eyes beaming down on me,
And then a window upward glide.

Fair as the morn, with rosy light,
She blushes with a faint surprise,
Then thinking of the previous night,
In dulcet tones she softly cries:

"It should have been put out by Nan,
But I'll be down within a minute—
No, never mind, leave your own can,
And put two quarts, please, in it."

Written in July 1897.

This poem was first published in the August 1901 issue of *National Magazine* in Boston. The poem is also referred to as "At Daybreak." In a letter to Edward Applegarth on September 15, 1898, London wrote the following: "'Je Ris Espoir' (sic) 'Hors de Saison' 'Day break' were experiments in feminine endings."

THE WORKER AND THE TRAMP

Heaven bless you, my friend—
    You, the man who won't sweat;
Here's a quarter to spend.

If you did but mend,
    My job you would get;—
Heaven bless you, my friend.—

On you I depend
    For my work, don't forget;—
Here's a quarter to spend.

Your course I commend,
    Nor regard with regret,—
Heaven bless you, my friend.

My hand I extend,
    For I love you, you bet:—
Here's a quarter to spend.

Ah! you comprehend
    That I owe a debt;
Heaven bless you, my friend,
Here's a quarter to spend.

Written in December 1898.

This poem was first published in the October 1901 issue of *The Comrade* in New York. It is also referred to as "The Workers Tribute to the Tramp." This form of poetry is called a villanelle.

LOVERS LITURGY

Ah! my brothers, we are mortals,
  Atoms on Time's ebb and flow,
Soon we pass the dreary portals,
  Soon to dreamless sleep we go;
We are sparkles, evanescent,
  Doomed to perish in the hour,
And our time is in the present,
  Ours but a moment's power.

Love, my brothers, is the essence,
  In the scheme of life and light;
Birth and death are fearful lessons—
  Out of darkness into night,—
Thus we flash, a moment's living,
  'Twixt the silent walls of death,
Flashing for a moment, giving
  Song but for a moment's breath.

Then that moment do not sadden,
  Prayers, nor beads, nor aves tell;
Then that moment do not madden
  With mad dreams of heaven or hell;
Trust that he who cast you idly,
  Asked of you nor aye nor nay,
Flung you idly, wildly, widely,
  For his whim will not ask pay.

For a whim of bubble-blowing,
  Perhaps to while an empty day,
For a whim of stubble-sowing,
  For a game at godlike play,
Shall the bubbles in the drifting,
  Pay the whim of Him who played?
Shall the seedlets in the shifting,
  Of the sifter be afraid?

Shall the playthings of a master,
  Falling idly from his hand,
Meet with meritless disaster,
  Meet with unearned reprimand?

Shall the children of a fancy,
   Born a certain race to run,
By an absurd necromancy,
   Penance pay when it is done?

O, my brothers, go not questing
   For some mystic grail in vain—
Why should ye a Master's jesting,
   Strive to fathom or make plain?
Wake ye from your fevered dreaming,
   Groping for forbidden toys,
All about you life is teeming,
   Singing of ungarnered joys.

Surely He who somewhere hovers,
   'Yond the reach of mortal ken,
Gazing down on love and lovers,
   Cannot blame the sons of men;
Cannot blame his bubbles bursting,
   Heart to heart and lips to lips;
Cannot blame his seedlets thirsting
   For the dew of honeyed lips.

Then again the golden chalice,
   Once again a lingering draught;
Surely He will bear no malice
   For the pledge divinely quaffed.
Thus, with sweet and fond caresses,
   Hearts that beat with mutual bliss,
He who loves is he who blesses,
   Sealing heaven with a kiss.

Written on January 15, 1899.

This poem was first published in the February 1901 issue of *The Raven* in Oakland.

HE CHORTLED WITH GLEE

He chortled with glee
As he read me the letter—
And why shouldn't he?
He chortled with glee,
'Twas a boy, you see,
And she was much better.
He chortled with glee
As he read me the letter.

Written on January 23, 1899.

This poem was first published in *Town Topics* in New York on April 20, 1899. This poem is a triolet.

WHEN HE CAME IN

When he came in
Why, I was out;
To borrow some tin
Was why he came in,
And I had to grin,
For he went without;
So I was in
And he was out.

Written on January 23, 1899.

This poem was first published in *Town Topics* in New York on April 26, 1899. It was reprinted in London's book *Martin Eden* (1909) (altered form, page 118) and also again in *Town Topics* on May 10, 1910 as "In and Out." The poem is a triolet.

IF I WERE GOD

If I were God one hour
    And, gazing down from heaven's dizzy stair,
Should see you idling in the garden there;
    If I were God one hour,
And saw you flirting with that grinning cad—
Yes, flirting, don't deny!—why, I'd get mad;
I'd loose the bolts of my almighty wrath
And turn the wretch to cinders in your path—
    If I were God one hour.

If I were God one hour
    And saw you in that garden, fair and tall,
I'm sure I'd fail to watch the sparrows fall;
    If I were God one hour,
And haply you should raise your eyes to mine,
Right then and there I know that I'd resign
And fling away my scepter, dearest Nan,
Descend to earth and make myself a man—
    If I were God one hour.

Written on January 23, 1899.

This poem was first published in *Town Topics* in New York on May 11, 1899.

THE WAY OF WAR

Man primeval hurled a rock,
Torn with angry passions he;
To escape the which rude shock,
Foeman ducked behind a tree.

Man primeval made a spear,
Swift of death on battle field;
Foeman fashioned other gear,
Fought behind his hidebound shield.

Man mediaeval built a wall,
Said he didn't give a dam;
Foeman not put out at all,
Smashed it with a battering ram.

Man mediaeval, just for fun,
Made himself a coat of mail;
Foeman laughed and forged a gun,
Peppered him with iron hail.

Modern man bethought a change,
Cast more massive iron-plate;
Foeman just increased his range,
Tipped his ball to penetrate.

Modern man, with toil untold,
Deftly built torpedo boats;
Foeman launched "destroyers" bold,
Swept the seas of all that floats.

Future man—ah! who can say?—
May blow to smithereens our earth;
In the course of warrior play
Fling death across the heavens' girth.

Future man may hurl the stars,
Leash the comets, o'er-ride space,
Sear the universe with scars,
In the fight 'twixt race and race.

Yet foeman will be just as cute
Amid the rain of falling suns,
Leave the world by parachute,
And build ethereal forts and guns.

And when skies begin to fall
And foeman still will new invent—
Into a star-proof world he'll crawl,
Heaven insured from accident.

Written in February 1899.

This poem was first published in *Once a Week* in Oakland on October 27, 1906.

SONNET

A Trumpet call, a bursting of the sod,
   And lo! I flung aside the clinging clay
   Lifted my flight along the star-strewn way
Among the white-robed saints that fled to God.
And he that held the gate, with holy nod,
   Did bid me enter that my feet might stray
   Amid the flowers with those that God obey;
The just, the good, and pure on earth there trod.

Dear heart: I questioned him if thou wert there,
   One of that bright-browed throng whose voices led
   The heavenly hymn of praise, the wondrous strain
That kissed in ecstasy the trembling air?
   But he that held the gate did shake his head,
   Thou wast not there; I turned away again.

Written in May 1899.

This poem was first published in February 1901 issue of *Dilettante* in Oakland.

SEA SPRITE AND THE SHOOTING STAR

A little sea sprite,
On the sea one night,
Cried "Now is the time for me,"
And he looked above,
And he looked for his love;
For he was in love, you see.

But his love was a star
In the sky a-far,
And she knew not his love so true;
So he tried to think
Of a magic link
'Twixt the sea and the sky so blue.

Then out of the sky,
From the moon on high,
A silvery moonbeam fell;
And it fell on the brine,
With its wonderful shine,
On the brine where the sea sprites dwell.

Though the siren sing
Where the sea bells ring
And the sleepy poppies dream—
Though the sea sprite knew
Their songs untrue,
He knew not the false moonbeam.

For the way seemed clear
To his love so dear,
And he needn't have wings to fly;
Up its silvery stream
He would climb by the beam,
He would climb right into the sky.

Up the glittering step
He carefully crept,
While his heart beat a merry tune;
But O what a fright
To the poor little sprite,
When he came to the crescent moon.

Alas! and a-lack!
He couldn't get back,
For the moonbeams flew away;
And the stars in the sky
Knew not he was nigh,
Or that he had lost his way.

There he sat forlorn,
On the crescent horn,
And thought of his home in the sea
Of his brothers at play
All the livelong day
On the foam so fresh and free.

Then he saw his star,
In her golden car,
As she twinkled above his head;
And he sobbed and sighed,
And woefully cried
That he wished—he wished he was dead.

But the little the star heard
His every word,
And thrilled at his musical voice
Like the tinkling of bells,
Or the songs of shells,
And it bade her heart rejoice.

For she was lonely and sad,
And no lover had;
And she'd twinkled so long up there,
It had often been said
That she never would wed—
And yet she was wonderous fair.

But often she'd seen,
On the ocean green,
The sea sprite who had loved her so;
Though he came not to woo,
She had loved him too,
Yet she never would tell him—oh no.

But as she looked down
On the lover she'd found—
The story is strange to relate—
She sprang from her car,
For the height was no bar,
And hurried to join her mate.

Oh how her heart beat,
As she leaped from her seat,
And fell to the moon below;
And the stars were aghast,
As she darted past,
And they all said "I told you so."

And her golden hair,
As she fell through the air,
Shown bright like a comet's tail;
While the people on earth,
All ceased from their mirth
As they watched her fiery trail.

Not a bit too soon,
She came to the moon,
Where she grasped her lover's hand;
And they sang with glee,
As they splashed in the sea,
Right into the sea sprite's land.

And the sea o' nights
Is bright with lights,
Whenever they're out to play
For the white sea foam
Is their beautiful home,
Where they live forever and aye.

Written in August 1899.

In a September 18, 1900 letter to Charles S. Pratt, co-Editor of *Little Folks* magazine, London wrote: "'The Sea Sprite' is an ancient effort, and chiefly an interest to me because of its almost countless refusals. Of all my work, it is, in that particular my banner Ms. Each rejection is a birthday, and my love grows with its birthdays." It was privately printed by R. W. Francis via the Keesling Press in Campbell, California in November 1932.

IN A YEAR

In a year, in a year, when the grapes are ripe,
I shall stay no more away—
Then if you still are true, my love,
It will be our wedding day.

In a year, in a year, when my time is past—
Then I'll live in your love for aye.
Then if you still are true, my love,
It will be our wedding day.

Written prior to 1901.

It is not known when London wrote this poem but it was first published in *The California Birthday Book*, Arroyo Press Guild, Los Angeles in January 1901.

A PASSIONATE AUTHOR TO HIS LOVE

Come write to me and be my Love,
And we will all the profits prove
That furnace sighings, signed and sealed,
And vows epistolary yield.

Empty the coffers of thy heart;
Its every throb and thrill impart;
Search every secret, holy nook;
'Twill make, Sweetheart, a lovely book.

And I will make thee, vow for vow,
And in my letters mention how
By thoughts of thee I'm sweetly harried,
Despite the fact that I am married.

Thou'lt write how to my arms thou'dst fly
If 'twere not for the legal tie;
And I how straight I'd fly to thee
If from my fetters I were free.

These tender things we'll put in print.
Sweetheart there may be millions in't!
The public simply can't resist
"Love Letters of a Socialist."

We'll turn our passion to account,
And realize a large amount.
If the plan thou dost approve
Come write to me and be my Love.

Written probably in late 1902 or early 1903.

This parody of Christopher Marlowe's "A Passionate Shepard to His Love" was inspired by Anna Strunsky, with whom London co-authored *The Kempton-Wace Letters*. A typescript copy of this poem is pasted inside London's copy of this book that is part of the Huntington Library's collection. London probably originally intended to only use this poem as a book inscription, but he later published it in *Recreation* in September 1904 under the pseudonym "Puck." The author is indebted to Jay Williams for his noting the omission of this poem from the first edition of this book.

ABALONE SONG

Oh, some folks boast of quail on toast
Because they think it's tony;
But I'm content to owe my rent
And live on abalone.

Oh! Mission Point's a friendly joint,
Where every crab's a crony,
And true and kind you'll ever find
The clinging abalone.

He wanders free beside the sea,
Where 'er the coast is stony;
He flaps his wings and madly sings—
The plaintive abalone.

Some stick to biz, some flirt with Liz
Down on the sands of Coney;
But we, by hell, stay in Carmel,
And whang the abalone.

We sit around and gaily pound,
And bear no acrimony,
Because our ob—ject is a gob
Of sizzling abalone.

Oh! some like ham and some like lamb,
And some like macaroni;
But bring me in a pail of gin
And a tub of abalone.

Oh! some drink rain and some champagne
Or brandy by the pony;
But I will try a little rye
With a dash of abalone.

Some live on hope and some on dope,
And some on alimony;
But our tom-cat, he lives on fat
And tender abalone.

The more we take, the more they make
In deep-sea matrimony;
Race suicide cannot betide
The fertile abalone.

Written about 1905.

This is a traditional song sung as one pounds abalone in preparation for eating. In 1905 London was a guest of George Sterling in Caramel, California where he and Sterling and Ambrose Bierce, among others, improvised lyrics as they pounded abalone. London first published these verses in *The Valley of the Moon* in October 1913 (Stanzas 1-4 on pages 386-387, stanza 5 on page 391, stanzas 6-9 on page 392). It is not known with certainty which verses were composed by London.

OF MAN OF THE FUTURE

Of man of the future! Who is able to describe him?
Perhaps he breaks our globe into fragments
In a time of warlike games.
Perhaps he hurls death through the firmament.
Man of the future! He is able to aim at the stars,
To harness the comets,
And to travel in space among the planets.

Written before 1915.

It is not known when London wrote this poem, but it was first published in Russian in *Komsomol Pravda*, Moscow on September 20, 1959. It first appeared in English in *Jack London and the Klondike* by Franklin Walker in 1966.

ON THE FACE OF THE EARTH YOU ARE THE ONE

I am your Adam, you are my Eve,
As in the days of old,
Just like Adam, he loved his Eve,
My love for you is bold,
My eyes are blinded by love that's true,
I see no one in this world but you,
Sweetheart divine,
Say you'll be mine,
I love you, you, you,

Chorus

On the face of the earth you are the one,
My one, only one, only one,
You are my love,
Like the sun up above,
Only one, only one, only one—dear,
Since the birth of the earth you are one,
My battle of love has begun,
I'll answer your calls,
Till life's curtain falls,
On the face of the earth you are one. one.

I strolled 'mongst flowers, I picked a rose,
That was my vision so true,
Among all those flowers,
One flower I chose, The rose, I chose, was you,
I longed for you since the world began.
I'll long for you till the end of man,
A vision of you,
Is my whole life's view,
I love you, you, you,

Chorus

Written before 1915.

This is a song lyric version of the poem, "On the Face of the Earth," which likely was not written by London. The lyrics, which are credited to him, are so trite that there is good reason to believe that he merely lent his name to them in exchange for a licensing fee. London had done this previously with respect to several stage plays for producers eager to capitalize on his name. They are included in this collection in the interest of comprehensiveness, and because they demonstrate London's continuing interest in music, his "first love."

This song was probably written shortly before it was published in 1915 by the Melodius Music Company in Boston, Mass. The sheet music is imprinted "Lyrics by Jack London and Music by Hassack Kubanoff and Joseph Riseman."

TICK! TICK! TICK!

Chorus

And the clock went, tick, tick, tick,
While she'd rest her little head on his shoulder,
And they'd kiss so quick, quick, quick,
And oh, how tight he'd hold her.
T'was a lovely trick, trick, trick,
And they played it oh so slick.
When the clock, went tick, then his heart, went click,
And it ended in a quick, slick, tick, tick, tick.

Written before 1915.

This song was probably written shortly before it was published in 1915 by the Melodius Music Company in Boston, Mass. The sheet music is imprinted "Lyrics by Jack London and Music by Hassack Kubanoff and Joseph Riseman." Only a promotional copy containing the chorus was available.

OH YOU EVERYBODY'S GIRL

Billy met a girlie, he learned to love her so,
He took her out to supper, and dough on her did blow,

… … … … …

Billie loved this girlie, indeed he did confess,
All mornin' noon and night__her picture he'd caress,

… … … … …

Written before 1915.

This song was probably written shortly before it was published in 1915 by the Melodius Music Company in Boston, Mass. The sheet music is imprinted "Lyrics by Jack London and Music by Joseph Riseman." Only a promotional copy containing the first page was available.

Portrait of young Jack London by Andrew J. Mill, San Jose.

SECTION B

JACK LONDON'S

UNPUBLISHED POETRY

The poems in this section are presented in the order in which they were written (when known).

In addition to the poems printed here for the first time, London's notes mention five other poems that he wrote:

"Still Hunt"
"Rich Morsels"
"Thlinket Anger"
"Future Wars"
"My Gentle Nurse"

No copies of these have been found to date.

GOLD

    Strange was the alchemy through which you passed,
    Before, deep-sunk in earth and massive rock,
    Thou layest concealed whilst centuries o'er thee passed;
    Nor felt the rush of life, the toil, the shock
    Of man above thee torn with emotions wild—
    Living, dying, existing but a space;
    Enduring sorrows or with joys beguiled;
    Crushing his fellows in that fierce onward race,
Where brute survived and true nobility was lost;
Where souls pursuing hot desire were passion tost.

    In cosmos vague, mysterious, unknown,
    'Mid elemental war pregnant with life,
    Where valleys fell and mountains were upthrown,
    Wert thou vanquished and banished from the strife. .
    Crushed 'neath a weight of overwhelming earth,
    The struggle o'er thee ceaselessly did wage;
    But thou didst sleep and wait thy second birth,
    When, with the strange, ungrateful genie's rage,
Who swore to slay the first that loosed him, gave him light,
Didst thou mankind with fierce, unholy avarice smite.

    As in the fabled tales of ancient days,
    Within a casket were imprisoned ills,
    The lid of which Pandora fain did raise,
    So wert thou guarded by the silent hills.
    Till one, more brave or curious than the rest,
    Cast wide your portals, let the light of day
    Behold the future goal of envious quest—
    The deadly drug to lure manhood away;
To steep in evanescent dreams the groping souls;
To cast them, 'wildered and forsaken, on treacherous shoals.

    The hot, incestuous love, the rude desire
    Of man for woman or of brute for brute,
    Were icebergs floating in a sea of fire,
    Contrasted with the agony acute,
    Which seized on man with love impure and base,
    When first beholding thee, he stood aghast,
    And felt within him shrivel up the grace,

The joy of perfect love before thy blast
Of all-consuming heat—hotter than that which wells
From crater mouths, or leaps from fond imagined hells.

   Yet wherein lies thy subtle, wondrous charm?
   The meteor flashing athwart the sky;
   The firefly in a summer evening's calm;
   Or meek glow-worm; thy warmest light outvie.
   Precious ? Art thou as rare, as true, as good,
   As she who blushes with the first surprise
   At conscious knowledge of her womanhood;
   Who glorious, peerless, hears with downcast eyes
And heaving breast, a lover's tale of love unfold,
Nor who, in that sweet moment, can her own withhold?

   Thou sprang'st into dominion, vast, supreme;
   Became the lodestar of man's pathless sea—
   The dreamer, 'wakening from his happy dream,
   Returns to earth, beholds and chases thee:
   The youth whose scheme of life has just begun;
   The man who walks erect in manhood's prime;
   The aged one whose race is nearly run;
   Forget the aim of life, the thought sublime,
And stifling conscience, yielding to covetous thirst,
Seek thee, and seeking, fall, degraded and accurst.

Completed in May 1897.

The text was taken from a manuscript at Stanford University. In a September 15, 1898 letter to Edward Applegarth, London wrote the following:
> "'Gold,' strange to say was just being written when I left—It was my first & only flight. You will see that I attempted an improvement on the 'Spenserian Stanza' by adding a second Iambic hexameter verse."

In a November 27, 1898 letter to Mabel Applegarth, London had the following to say about this poem:
> "Why, that poem on gold is one of the finest object-lessons in my possession. I was ambitious in that. With no more comprehension of the aims and principles of poetry, than a crab, I proposed or rather, purposed to make something which would be something. I would strike out on new trails; I would improve on the Spencerian Stanza; I would turn things upside down. So I tried what has been probably tried a thousand times and discarded because it was worthless; one Alexandrine at the end of the stanza was not enough; I added a second. I treated my theme as Dryden or Thompson would have treated it. My elephantine diction was super—I out-Johnsoned Johnson. I was a fool and no one to tell me."

JE VIS EN ESPOIR

I live in hope from day to day,
Of a joyous consummation;
When all my friends in manner gay,
Give me congratulation.

I live in hope that quick the hour,
Still in the dim perspective,
Shall me all happiness endower,
And cease to be subjective.

I live in hope that bells shall ring
In peals magnificent,
And to me tidings haply bring
From fate omnipotent

I live in hope the day to see,
When with a thrill electric,
I'll merry hail with greatest glee,
A victory majestic.

My hope is this: that there may pass,
An uncle wisely provident,
From earth, who great wealth did amass.
And leave it me, an indigent.

Completed in May 1897.

The text was taken from a manuscript at Stanford University. In a letter to Edward Applegarth on September 15, 1898, London wrote the following: "'Je Ris Espoir' (sic) 'Hors de Saison' 'Day break' were experiments in feminine endings."

MY CONFESSION

I love to feel the wind's great power
On my silken sails on high;
As I upon my ivied tower
My Dragon Kite do fly.

Each gusty breeze that stirs the trees
Strikes on my silken kite
Sending melodies like these
Down from the living light.

The silken string (a dainty thing,
And white and bright and neat),
I fasten to a phonograph
And make the breezes speak.

That's how I write my stories,
The wind upon the string
Makes clear the sun-sky glories
And tells me everything.

Completed in May 1897.

The text was taken from a manuscript at the Oakland Public Library.

THE SOCIALIST DREAM

The room was narrow and cold and grim;
He reigned supreme, a king of dirt;
Beneath a slouched hat's shadowed brim,
He viewed the kingdom about him girt:
But thoughts he held of fairer mold
Than filth and stench so manifold.

Vanished the press of misery,
The stamp of vice and poverty's face,
The scenes he was so used to see,
The things so low, so vile, so base:
For dreaming, did he a long behold,
Where truth was worshipped as of old.

A land of honesty and thrift,
Where labor had its due reward;
Where each applied his special gift;
Nor turned from plowshare unto sword
To rob his neighbor of his gold,
But worked him weal instead of wold.

He saw the soil enriched by men,
Who gloried in such honest life,
Ranking with those of greater ken
Whose pleasures were in mental strife;
But who, as comrades true and bold,
Were in man's brotherhood enrolled.

He heard the hum of joy arise
From merry hearts and housefires bright;
A joy, that climbing, scaled the skies,
And cried "Rejoice! There is no night!"—
'Twas but a melody uprolled
Of souls secure within the fold.

Truth and honor were upraised,
And purity of thought and deed.
The multitudes, adoring, gazed,
And in their hearts received the seed;

And righteousness, with firmest hold,
Sweet truths and many to them told.

The vision fair, before him shone;
His heart in ecstasies was rapt;
He awoke—he was no more alone,
For some one had quite loudly tapped:
The door was op'ed and in there strolled
A woman of demeanor cold.

"Your rent is due," this female said.
"'Tis due these many, many days:
Your lazy body I have fed—
Say! How much can you raise?
Nay, not in looks so fierce and bold,
But in bright silver or hard gold."

The socialist, in accents mild,
Told her a lie upon the spot,
And her soft soul with ease beguiled
Of treasure wondrous he had got:
His aunt had died; the bells had tolled;
His was the money; hers the mould.

Then hied him to a laboring man—
Forgotten was his vision pure—
Whose hand was rough and face was wan,
And did a greater lie conjure.
The man from his scant pittance doled
The price for which the lie was sold.

The visionare in pleasure spent,
Regardless of his dream so bright,
The money which his friend had lent;
Beholding 'mid a magic light
The fond utopia unrolled,
Of which the seers so often told.

Vanished all sin and foul desire;
Forgotten were deeds low and base;
Nor thinking of their vengeful ire,
He walked amid another race

Of men who ne'er their friends cajoled,
But truth and virtue did uphold.

'Tis thus with all poor mortals here,
Whose dual natures struggles wage;
Who for misfortune drop a tear,
Then in the war of life engage,
And with their passions uncontrolled,
Rage on in wild pursuit of gold.

Completed in May 1897.

The text was taken from a manuscript at the University of Southern California. In a letter to Edward Applegarth on September 15, 1898, London wrote the following: "'Socialist Dream' was first attempt to merely think in meter—full of errors."

HORS DE SAISON

Nothing but comes too late with me,
No matter how I reason;
The fashions swiftly from me flee;
I'm always out of season.

My slim income with care I eke,
To gratify some passion;
But when I do it is antique,
Having gone out of fashion.

I struggle 'mid temptations great,
To take a brief vacation;
But upward climbs the railroad rate,
'Yond all anticipation.

When at the seaside I arrive,
The crowd is in the city;
No matter how I do contrive,
I miss them—more's the pity.

I never bought the latest hat,
Nor other 'bomination;
But that my friends said "Look at that,
It's older than creation."

And thus it is with all my clothes;
My neckties, trousers, waistcoats;
My cuffs, my studs, my shoes, my hose;
My summer suits and greatcoats.

I learned to waltz with hop and jump;
And then the dancers glided;
My friends thought me the biggest chump,
And all my 'tempts derided.

The cigarette I learned to smoke
With nausea most horrible;
But custom changed with one fell stroke
To briarwood pipes intolerable.

In. politics it is the same;
When tariff-struck, hilaric,
'Gainst free trade's evils I disclaim,
The crowd's gone bimetallic.

I never loved but that too late
I plead my adoration:
Another man had been there first,
To my great consternation.

At last one day, cursing my fate,
In dark despair to 'scape her,
'Twas told me on the brink, "Too late,
Suicide's no more the caper."

Nothing but comes too late with me,
No matter how I reason;
The fashions swiftly from me flee;
I'm always out of season.

Completed in July 1897.

The text was taken from a manuscript at the Stanford University. In a letter to Edward Applegarth on September 15, 1898, London wrote the following: "'Je Ris Espoir' (sic) 'Hors de Saison' 'Day break' were experiments in feminine endings." According to London's manuscript log, this poem was submitted to: "Judge—July 12/97 Harpers—Mar. 15/99 Kellogg Syn—Mar. 31/99 N.Y. Sun—Apr. 12/99."

HE NEVER TRIED AGAIN

(With apologies to Henry of England)

He heard the wondrous tale and went
    To Klondyke's golden shore;
A year of trial and toil he spent,
    And found not gold galore.
And starved and frozen he returned,
    Singing a sad refrain;
For nuggets he no longer yearned—
    He never tried again.

The air rang loud with war's alarms,
    And a soldier he became;
But Romance soon lost all her charms,
    And life in camp was tame.
The drill was stiff, the grub was bad;
    He slept out in the rain;
His captain was a beastly cad—
    He never tried again.

He met a pretty Summer Girl,
    Who stole his heart away;
She was a precious little pearl
    And could not say him nay.
But when he asked her for her heart,
    She searched and searched in vain;
For sad to say she had no heart—
    He never tried again.

Three times he'd tried, three times he'd failed;
    It could not last alway;
On Harlem Bridge he wept and wailed,
    And leaped into the bay.
The water cold, he called for aid,
    And struggled might and main;
He could not swim, so there he stayed—
    He never tried again.

Completed on October 1, 1898.

The text was taken from a manuscript at the Huntington Library. According to London's manuscript log, this poem was submitted to: "Chronicle Oct. 1/99 Inter Ocean—Oct. 5/99."

THE KLONDYKER'S DREAM

(With all respects to the "Mariner")

In slumbers of midnight the Klondyker lay;
The snow was fast falling, the cold was intense;
But weary and hungry, his cares flew away,
And visions of dinners were calling him hence.

He dreamed of his home, of the dining-room table,
And servants that waited his every behest;
He longed O to eat, to eat all he was able,
For ah! of all dreams he had dreamed 'twas the best.

Then Fancy her marvelous miracles wrought,
And bade the thin starved one get out of his bed;
The Klondyke he left far behind him, he sought
The place where the hungered could always be fed.

He came in good season, the table was laid;
The rich, fragrant coffee was steaming and hot;
The pastries and puddings were there all arrayed;
The beefsteak was done, aye was done to a dot.

His fingers were trembling, so rich was the fare,
And when Grace was ended he murmured Amen!
And took, of all dishes, the beefsteak so rare;
Ah! he was the happiest man of all men.

The jaws of the sleeper are moving with joy;
Food quickens his palate, his hardships seem o'er;
A feeling of plenty steals over the boy—
"O God! thou hast fed me, I ask for no more."

Ah! whence is that form which now bursts on his eye?
Ah! what is that sound that now catches his ear?
'Tis the dog of the Klondyke thieving so sly!
'Tis a crunching of jaws, a crunching quite near!

He springs from the blankets, he seizes his gun;
Gaunt Famine confronts him with images dire;

But out of the tent goes the dog on the run,
For well he knows when it's time to retire.

The last piece of bacon is gone from the sack;
He weeps, O he weeps, for he knows what it means;
The last piece of bacon—'twill never come back;
Henceforth his diet must be sour bread and beans.

O Klondyker, woe to thy dreams of good fare!
In waking they left thee, they left on the fly;
Where now is that beefsteak so juicy and rare;
The coffee, the pudding, the pastry and pie?

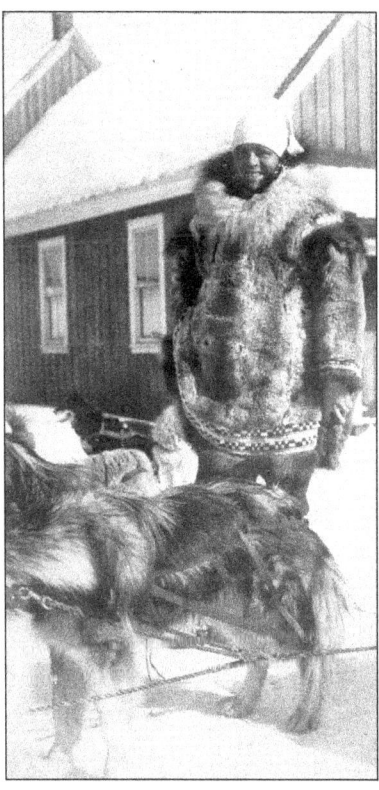

Jack London fully dressed for the "Klondike," with dogs and sled, but the photograph was actually taken during a race held at Truckee, California, in 1915..

Completed on October 1, 1898.

The text was taken from a manuscript at the Huntington Library.

MOODS

Who has not laughed with the skylark,
And bid his heart rejoice?
Laughed till the mirth-loving heavens
Echoed his laughter back?
Joyed in the sheer joy of living,
And sung with gladsome voice,
Lays that were cheerful and merry,
And bid his heart rejoice?

Who has not frowned in the gloaming,
And felt the skies grow black;
While o'er him spread the dark mantle
Of sullen, solemn Gloom,
Whose mutterings broke the silence
Like echoes from the tomb—
Like echoes of lost endeavors—
Reproaches from the tomb?

Who has not cursed in his passion,
As Anger's stinging lash,
Biting and smarting and racking,
Fell on his naked back?
Felt in his veins feverish tumult,
The strife, the savage clash,
As when hot steel, leaped from the scabbard,
Meets steel with crash on crash?

Who has not wept in his sorrow,
And looked in vain for morn;
Waiting with hopeless yearning,
The sun from out the bourn?
Heard from the world the sad sobbing
Of Faith and Hope forlorn?
Known that the sun had forever
Gone down into the bourn?

Completed on October 5, 1898.

The text was taken from a manuscript at the Huntington Library. According to London's manuscript log, this poem was submitted to: "*Overland Monthly—* October 5, 1899."

CUPID'S DEAL

"Me tell your fortune? Nay' " she cried;
And then, in mood relenting,
And roughish air, was by my side—
"And mind, there's no resenting.
The things I tell are true as true
As ever yet were told to you
By gifted seer or Gypsy crew—
Don't think that I'm inventing."

"First make your wish, but don't tell me,"
(Ah well she knew my yearning)
"For then I can't tell true, you see;
Some things are past discerning.
But what is this? A lady fair,
Of sprightly mien and debonair—
Next Five of Clubs, which means beware!"
(Ah me, my ears are burning)

"And then yourself, the Knave of Hearts,
In dangerous conjunction
With Cupid's ace, who aims his darts
At you without compunction.
Twixt you and her he bends his bow—
And my advice? 'Tis that you go
To Cupid's Court, and bending low,
Pray him for an injunction.

"Your fortune's told, I see no more;
The cards are counterpointing;
But hold' What's this? Within a Four?
Regarding an appointing? —
'Tis on its way, 'Twill come to you,
A sweetly scented <u>billet-doux</u>,
A very charming <u>Billet-doux</u>,
And very disappointing.

"Your wish is blank; but for the rest,
Remember what's foretold you,
And—nay, you must not, shan't protest,
And say that I've cajoled you.

Come sir, confess; you can't deny
The truths which I have given—why
The cards say so." And I reply,
"I'd like to know who told you."

And this is how it all began,
And why she called me "Mister";
For she was at the depot when
I'd gone to meet my sister.
Because she did not know her, she
Thought the very worst of me—
That is—I—Well I kissed her.

Completed on October 8, 1898.

The text was taken from a manuscript at Utah State University. According to London's manuscript log, this poem was submitted to: "*Overland Monthly*—Oct. 5/99."

REPUBLICAN BATTLE-HYMN

O Fathers of the Nation,
    We struggle in thy name;
Each man was at his station
    Ere yet the summons came.
We felt our country calling,
    And sprang into the fray—
O in thy might appalling,
    Withhold not victory.

We ask that right be given,
    And justice where 'tis due;
Reward for those who've striven
    And did the best they knew.
But punish those, who lying,
    Have wrought thee evil deeds;
And pardon those denying,
    Who follow other creeds.

Our country is far dearer
    Than closer bonds of blood;
For we would see far clearer,
    The nation's common good.
Enlighten thou our labor;
    Invest us with thy might;
So that we may not waver
    While battling for the right.

We would our country flourished;
    That all may at her breast,
Suckling as babes, be nourished,
    Nor fail in fruitless quest;
That she, our mighty mother,
    Will see the day come by,
When man calls man "O brother!"
    And all shall know the tie.

O Fathers of the Nation,
    We struggle in thy name;
Each man was at his station
    Ere yet the summons came.

We felt our country calling,
   And sprang into the fray—
O in thy might appalling,
   Withhold not victory.

Completed on October 21, 1898.

The text was taken from a manuscript at the Huntington Library. This song and the following one were submitted in a writing contest sponsored by the Republican Party of Oakland. One of them (it's not clear which) won a prize of $10.00.

REPUBLICAN RALLYING SONG

(Air of "Marching Through Georgia")

Gathered round our standards, boys, we face the fray again;
We have gathered in our might and here we will remain,
Till we win to victory and sweep the whole campaign,
While we are counting majorities.

(Chorus)

Hurrah! Hurrah! Our platform's here to stay!
Hurray! Hurray! O hear the donkeys bray!
Won't they sing another song before we go away!
While we are counting majorities.

To the next election, boys, 'twill find us side by side;
To the Grand Old Party, boys, its men so true and tried:
Let the toast go round the board and drink it in all pride,
While we are counting majorities.

(Chorus)

We've a candidate who'll win, or else his name's not GAGE;
He will put the "Little Giant" in a little cage—
Won't he make them gnash their teeth and kick themselves with rage,
While we are counting majorities.

(Chorus)

There is something coming, boys, we feel it in the air;
'Tis a tidal wave that's made to mash them 'yond repair—
Where will we be at? Oho! You bet we'll all be there,
While we are counting majorities.

(Chorus)

When election day has come we'll vote our ticket straight;
Then will they be out of it for all they feel so great—
We won't do a thing to them but rub them off the slate,
While we are counting majorities.

(Chorus)

Completed on October 21, 1898.

The text was taken from a manuscript at the Huntington Library.

MY LITTLE PALMIST

The leaves stirred softly overhead,
While from my hand a tale was read,
By laughing lips of rosy red;
My little Palmist.
O that slight form so dainty-fair,
That pulsing breast, beyond compare,
That cadenced rise and fall of air!—
Of breaths the balm'est.

"This line, unbroken, deep and long,
Assurance gives of health most strong,
And truely 'twill thy days prolong;
The line Vitalis.
While this, so clear and firm and fine,
Says Cupid's toils about thee twine,
And happiest wedlock will be thine—
'Tis called Mensalis.

"And here, thy disposition gay,
Is quickly learned from lines which say,
That where you go or where you stay,
Your ways are jolly.
And yet again, these furrows blent,
One thing alone for thee is meant,
In Love's fond dalliance you've spent
Fair hours in folly.

"By this, and this, and this, is told,
Good friends about thee are enrolled,
While Love's delights, so manifold,
Thy life shall gladden.
Nor sudden sorrow, or swift pain,
Nor misery shall thee enchain;
Nor blighting curse, or dread murrain,
Thy heart shall sadden.

"Yet least among thy pleasures great,
There will a little maiden wait,
With love, as bird feels for its mate,
With love sincerest."

Ere yet she ceased, I knelt, a thrall,
As to my heart her last words fall,—
"I've held naught back, so this is all,
For thee, my Dearest."

O sweet that rippling flow of sound,
That fairy speech which wrapped me 'round!—
Those magic meshes 'bout me bound,
I would not sever.
O sweet those pure, pellucid eyes,
Whose slightest glance I fondly prize!—
Ah God! in this, my paradise,
I'd stay forever.

It seems but yesterday that we,
With hand in hand, and knee to knee,
Spent one sweet hour in childish glee;
My little Palmist.
But yesterday,—Ah well-a-day!
And where is now my little fay,
Who scanned my hand and went away?
O sing thou Psalmist.

Completed on November 1, 1898.

The text was taken from a manuscript at Utah State University. According to London's manuscript log, this poem was submitted to: "Munsey's—Nov. 1/99."

BALLADE OF THE FALSE LOVER

He asked me there to be his bride,
O long and long ago;
He drew me close, my tears he dried,
His face was all aglow;
And I, poor me! how could I show
My love? What could I say?
I lay upon his breast—and lo,
He kissed and rode away.

He spoke me fair, and from my side,
He swore he would not go;
Said Heaven nor Hell could not divide
Us, for he loved me so.
Ah woe is me, I did not know,
I could not say him nay;
I lay upon his breast—and lo,
He kissed and rode away.

There lost I both my heart and pride,
And all I could bestow;
For when he looked and longed and sighed,
My tongue would not say no;
And when he whispered, soft and low,
That I was his for aye,
I lay upon his breast—and lo,
He kissed and rode away.

        Envoi

Sister, 'twas thus: I did not know,
Nor dream that love would stray;
I lay upon his breast—and lo,
He kissed and rode away.

Completed on November 16, 1898.

London also refers to this poem as "He Kissed and Rode Away." The text was taken from a manuscript at the Oakland Public Library.

RETURN OF ULYSSES—A MODERN VERSION

Scene:—a club lounging room.

George (*Just back from Klondike*)
Jack (*invalided from Manila*)
Harry (*who stayed at home*)

(*Enter George and Harry by opposite doors*)

Harry (*with hearty surprise*)

By Jove! It's George—this is a joy!

George (*as they grip hands*)

How goes it any way, old boy?
You're looking well—how wags the town?
And you? It's time you've settled down?

Harry

I have, old man; no more abroad,
The wee sma' hours—

George

Say, how is Maud?
You know, Miss Smith, that slim brunette—
Remember on the parapet
How she and I made poor Jack sweat?
Yes, yes, I know, it was a sin,
But then I had my doubts of him;
She liked me best, as you'll allow,
Better than all the rest. And now—
Well, I shall try my luck to-night,
Pay her a call; if all goes right
You'll be best man—there, there, don't scold,
I know you will do that for—

Harry

Hold!
You do not understand; let me
Explain. You see—I—that is—we—

(*Enter Jack, who pounces upon them effusively. All shake hands and clap each other on the shoulder.*)

Jack

How's Klondike, George? Let's heft your sack;
Of dust I hope you have no lack;
And Harry, here, who will not roam,
Our gorgeous, glorious stay-at-home—
How fares the world with you? Hast yet
A wife unto your hearth to fret
You to an early grave? But come,
The news,—(steward, your jolliest mumm)—
Who's born? who's dead? who's crossed the line?
The married? the divorced?—in fine,
The news, O man, the news. And say,
Er—Maud, Miss Smith, the little fay,
How is she? Is her name the same
As when I left?

George

Another flame!
Ha! Ha!

Jack

What! You! O, I forgot;
It's "I love you,
I love you not"—
A merry game for us to play,
In which, I wage, she'll say you nay.
Why you may have unmeasured gold,
But now-a-days, the soldier bold,
The hero of the camp and field,
Is all the rage; beneath his shield
Stalks Love, triumphant, and the fair
Can rest none other place than there,

Yes, they'll be wild over my scars,
Wild over me, just from the wars,
While you, who did a—mining go,
Tell me, what have you got to show?

George (*mock-heroically*)

Show? I? What have I got to show?
'Mid vasty wastes of Arctic snow,
Where blackness shrouds the silent world,
And death broods over all, I hurled
My challenge to the stars, unfurled
My standard and did mighty deeds.
I led a dozen wild stampedes;
I lived for months on moose-meat straight;
I froze my feet, nor did I wait
Their healing, till I froze my nose.
Aye, to great hazards I arose,
And had I proper speech to tell
My "ventures in that frozen hell,
I would your inmost soul affright
With deeds done by the Northern Light.
(descending to the colloquial manner)
Well, here I am, and I am rich,
Yea, in experience—the which
Will not advance my suit, you see.
But as for dust—between us three,
I'm broke, I haven't got a red;
And yet, I think, when all is said,
I stand as good a chance as you.
You went to war—how did you do
In way of gold? What is your wealth?
And further, how's your state of health?
You're looking yellow—<u>quid pro quo,</u>
Speak up, what have you got to show?

Jack

No more. I did not play polo
With Northern Lights below zero—
No, but I starved on the transports,
With empty stomach stormed the forts,

Or ate poor grub in poorer camp,
Shivered and shook out in the damp,
Was shot through arm, and thigh, and breast,
And caught a cold upon my chest,
Then fever claimed me for his own,
And I was invalided home.
So, like a gory son of Mars,
I've nothing else to show but scars.
And George, old chap, forgive me, do,
For my most foolish words to you;
We're comrades in misfortune, now,
And to her choice. Maud's choice, we'll bow,
And still be friends.

George (*as they shake hands*)

And one word more—
He who shall win the lady's door,
Shall recollect his friend forlorn,
And the proud hour of his first born
Shall see him praise and bless the same
By giving it his comrade's name.
Thus is our brotherhood begun,
And. he who wins or loses—

Jack (*wildly signalling the steward*)

Done!
What will—

Harry (*sarcastically*)

Suppose it is a girl?

Jack

That is the question of a churl—
We shall call her, and not man her,
Jacqueline or Georgiana.

George (*as the steward waits their order*)

Ye gods! Well done! An answer meet
For the occasion—'tis Harry's treat,
And treat you shall, before you go—
Besides, what have you got to show?

(*Harry rises to his feet and is followed by George and Jack.
The steward returns and they raise their glasses.*)

Harry

I stayed at home; I cannot show
War's ravages, nor Klondike's woe.
I've not gained much of which to boast,
But to yourselves I drink a toast:
Here's to Mars' son, who bravely stopped
A brace of Spanish balls—and dropped;
Here's to the son of Mammon, bold,
Wealthy in lore, if not in gold'
And now a health to the first born—
Here's to <u>her</u> god-papa forlorn;
Here's to <u>her</u> dad, who blessed the same
By giving <u>her</u> his rival's name;
And here's to Maud, the last of all—
Just shake the tree, she's sure to fall.

(*They laughingly drink and depart together; but before they
have gone a block, who do they meet but the very Maud in question.*)

Maud (*most graciously, as she extends both hands to George
and Jack, while Harry drops into the background.*)

What a surprise—both George and Jack—
I did not know that you were back.
Why Jack, how brown you are, and so—
Come up this evening—don't say no,
I'm home to you at any time,
That is if you will deign to climb—
We're living in a flat, you know.

(*She indicates Harry and lovingly takes his arm.
George and Jack act as though they had a pressing engagement.*)

Harry (*very modestly*)

And this is all I have to show.

Maud

Be sure and come —please don't forget.

Harry (*sotto voice*)

She'll wait in vain for them, I bet.
(*Exit, with Maud clinging to his arm.*)
(*Jack and George fall upon each other's breast.*)

Jack

Our Maud, our dainty Maud, is wed!

George

Woe! Woe! Our eldest born is dead!

(*Exit, limply.*)

Completed on December 12, 1898.

The text was taken from a manuscript at Stanford University. All notes and stage directions in parenthesis are presented here in italics but were not italicized in the original manuscript. According to London's manuscript log, this poem was submitted to: "Colliers Weekly—Dec. 5/99 Scroll—Dec. 20/99 Harpers—Jan. 3/99 The Western Press—Mar. 12/99 Am. Press Association—Mar. 31/99 Frank Leslies Weekly—Apr. 20/99."

RAINBOWS END

Just over the way where the rainbow fell,
I knew I would find a treasure of gold,
So I clambered over the fence pell mell,
Just over the way where the rainbow fell;
But I promised her I never would tell,
And I know if I tell you'll tell her I told.
Just over the way where the rainbow fell,
I certainly found a treasure of gold.

Completed on January 23, 1899.

London also referred to this triolet by its first verse. The text was taken from a manuscript at the Huntington Library. According to London's manuscript log, this poem was submitted to: "New England Magazine —Apr. 4/99 Vogue—May 18/99 Washington Star—June 2/99 Detroit Free Press—July 5/99."

HIS TRIP TO HADES

Trying to miss his trip to Hades,
Jack returned my umbrella;
Still you see I am afraid he's
Failed to miss his trip to Hades.
Mine? No, Some mistake he's made, he's
Borrowed from some other fellah,
Trying to miss his trip to Hades,
Jack returned my umbrella.

Completed on January 23, 1899.

The text of this triolet was taken from a manuscript at the Huntington Library. According to London's manuscript log, this poem was submitted to: "New England Magazine—Apr. 4/99 Vogue—May 18/99 Washington Star—June 2/99 Detroit Free Press—July 5/99 Boots & Shoes—July 19/99 Am. Press Ass—Aug. 15/99 Puck—Sep. 7/99 Sunday Globe—Sep. 12/99."

A HEART

    A lonely dwelling in a garden bowered,
Far from the world, the haunts of busy men,
It stood alone. No traveler yet had ventured
Down the shaded walk to where the door,
Scented with jessamine sweet and climbing rose,
Extended half a welcome, and again,
Half shyly turned away.
                And cradled here,
A home of pretty fancies and strange dreams,
It had beheld, untroubled, the nesting birds,
And flowering lawns and budding trees, and seen,
With blinded eyes, the scheme of life unfold;
Often it had wondered how the river met the sea,
And stealing glimpses of the far highway,
Had watched the hurrying forms and tried to guess
The deeds of valor or the remote lands
Which called them on and on and would not let
Them lift their eyes or idle by the way.
The languid hours had crept by unawares,
And years slipped into years until at last
The door was all a-tremble, like a ripe
Rose petal, fluttering to the wind's soft kiss;
And now there was a spirit of unrest
Through all its halls and inmost recesses,
A pulse of richer life and consciousness
Of things to come, a hum of preparation
As for a guest, unsummoned, yet expected.

    Once, a young wayfarer turned aside,
Lured by the noonday peace and pleasant shades,
And sought some quiet, fern-wreathed spot where he
Might rest his weary limbs and cool his brow.
But ló a swift turn in the walk disclosed
The house. Doffed was his plumed cap in awe
And slow amazement; he half turned, as though
It were a trespass, then his hand, quick-raised,
Lifted the latch to enter.
                Ah' the door
Was all but pressed ajar'
                But comrades called,

And minded him of other quests. The world
Shrilled keenly through the trees, and trumpets blared;
The latch fell softly and the garden knew
No more his presence; his proud plume was lost
Among the many thronged upon the highway.

    At last, all unannounced, the guest arrived;
Nor did he know whither the path did lead,
But with high pride, brushing aside the dew
And crushing under heel the scattered flowers,
He hastened toward the river's marge. A rose,
Swaying on dainty stem, essayed to bar
His passage, but, rough-flung, his mantle snapped
Her slender life and trailed her in the dust.
The waiting door received him, and the latch
Shot rudely upward to his heavy hand;
The shock aroused no echoes, but the rose
Which clung above let fall its ripened petals
In fluttering flakes of ruddy light. They fell
Unnoticed, for he thrust the door apart
And sounded down the hall with sweeping tread.

    'Twas plain that he had trod such halls before;
His bold eyes ranged unerringly to where
The shimmering gauze but told the secret which
It strove to hide, the entrance to the shrine,
The inner sanctuary where as yet
No priest had entered and no flame had burned.
Swift the strong hand, the veil was rent in twain,
He stood within the holiest of holies.
At first, the somber light and brooding calm,
Withheld him and he paused in reverent awe,
Abashed before a presence by whose side
His soul was dwarfed, and on his inner sight
There smote a consciousness of nobler things.
He turned, as to retrace his path, when ló
The air grew heavy with the perfumed freight
Of unseen censers and a mellow flood
Of rapturous music stole upon his ear,
Dim lamps awoke, the altar burst in flame,
A dazzling light, a mighty glory fell
Upon him and his soul was kissed with fire.

Yet he had kissed and thus been kissed before,
By many altars had he knelt and laid
Fat firstling lambs and lavish hecatombs,
In many shrines had waited till the dawn
Reddened the east and called him forth again.
And so he rested through the sweet long night,
And when the day awoke, aroused himself,
Stepped lightly o'er the shattered veil, nor thought
To bend his head in last obeisance;
Again he brushed aside the dew and crushed
The flowers; his laugh rang loud and he was gone.
'Twas then the flame upon the altar died.

   A lonely dwelling in a garden hidden,
Far from the world, the haunts of busy men,
It stands unknown. The walk where once He trod
Is weed-grown and the brambles bar the way;
No more the scent of jessamine or of rose
Lingers about the open door; chill winds
Go out and in, rustling sad memories,
Dead leaves and musty draperies of gauze.
The shrine is cold and lifeless, and the house
No longer dreams of things to come, nor waits
A guest. It still beholds the hurrying forms
Along the highway, but it does not question
Whence or whither, it has learned the quest
And knows the way the river meets the sea.

Completed in February 1899.

The text was taken from a manuscript at the Oakland Public Library. According to London's manuscript log, this poem was submitted to: "Pall Mall—Feb. 24/99 Lippencott's—Mar. 15/99 New Eng. Mag—Apr. 12/00 Atlantic Monthly—May 18/99 Ladies World—June 12/99 Ledger—July 5/99."

THE SONG OF THE FLAMES

We are motes of sunshine stolen
    When the world was fair and young,
Stolen from our joytime golden,
    Into earth's black bowels flung;
Kissed of light and born of passion,
    Thrilling with the wine of life,
Ravished in most cruel fashion,
    We were banished from the strife.

Pent in prisons dark and loathsome,
    Cells of sorrow, 'reft of mirth,
In our rocky chamber, lonesome,
    Slept we till our second birth,—
Slept we through the long, long ages,
    Dreaming of the time to be,
Till God, turning many pages,
    Deemed it fit to set us free.

Completed in March 1899.

The text was taken from a manuscript at the Huntington Library. According to London's manuscript log, this poem was submitted to: "Lippencott's—Mar. 15/99 New Eng. Mag.—Apr. 12/99 Atlantic Monthly—May 18/99 Munseys—June 10/99 N.Y. Sun—July 5/99 Independent—July 19/99 Criterion—Sept. 26/99."

THE GIFT OF GOD

I.

"Name me the gift of God!"
A man commanded.
His brow was furrowed
With thought.
He wished to know all things.

II.

There was a clamor among the peoples;
Many strove to answer,
And many were silent.
Some did not care,
Yet none were too busy to listen.
At first,
They named all things,
In loud voices,
Till the weak were hushed.

III.

Then the strong ones became as one:
"Life is the gift of God!" they cried,
In a mighty chant,
Which shook the heavens.
But in time,
They became tired,
And no longer outraged the sky.

IV.

Then a graybeard,
Doddering on the edge of his grave,
Raised a thin voice.
He had seen three generations
Come and go;
He knew all tricks;
He said, "Death is the gift of God."

He knew.
But the people were angry,
And in a great clamor,
Drowned his thin voice.

Completed on June 2, 1899.

The text was taken from a manuscript at the Oakland Public Library. According to London's manuscript log, this poem was submitted to: "Washington Star—June 2/99 Detroit Free Press—July 5/99 Independent—July 19/99 Town Topics—Sept. 26/99 ? Picayune—Nov. 1/99 Sunday Globe—Nov. 15/99 N.Y. Sun—Feb. 3/00."

MEMORY

Grim prompter of forgotten lines
With wings of sable night,
Stealing the light of day,
Why have you come
In this, my perfect port,

            O why?

            O why?

In this, my perfect port,
Why have you come
Stealing the light of day
With wings of sable night,
Grim prompter of forgotten lines.

Completed on June 2, 1899.

The text was taken from a manuscript at the Huntington Library. According to London's manuscript log, this poem was submitted to: "Washington Star—June 2/99 Atlantic Monthly—July 5/99 Independent—July 19/99 Criterion—Sept. 26/99 Sunday Globe—Nov. 15/99."

GEORGE STERLING

I saw a man open an iris petal.
He ran his finger underneath the edge,
unfolded it, and smoothed it out a little,
not as one guilty of a sacrilege—
because he knew flowers, and understood
that what he did would maybe help them grow—
though for a moment he was almost God.
Alone as we are, growing is so slow.
I think of one who tried like that to unfold
the margin of his life where it was curled,
to see into the shadows shot with gold
that lie in iris hues about the world.
Because he dared to touch the sacred rim,
does God resent this eagerness in him?

It is not known when this poem was completed.

The text of this poem was taken from a manuscript at the Huntington Library. George Sterling was a prominent California poet whose work London greatly admired. They developed a close personal relationship. In their correspondence London addressed him as "Greek" and signed himself as "Wolf." Sterling later moved to Carmel where he established an artists' enclave that London frequented and where they wrote "Abalone Song." London portrayed Sterling as Russ Brissenden in *Martin Eden* and as Mark Hall in *The Valley of the Moon*.

HOMELAND

I.

Beautiful Homeland, my own dear Homeland,
Deep in my heart dwells a love for Thee e–ver–more;
To Thee re–turning, my heart Is yearning,
For Thy great mountains. Thy peaceful green vales.
In many foreign lands a wanderer I strolled,
Oft have their wonders and their beauties been extolled;
But none can compare with Thee, oh fairest on earth
And none shall I love as Thee, O land of my birth . . . . . .
      Homeland . . . . . Homeland

Refrain:—

Beautiful Homeland, my own dear Homeland,
Where hearts are loyal and friendship is ever true;
Beautiful Homeland, my own dear Homeland,
Hope of all mankind that loves peace and freedom;
Embraced by oceans and God's sunny skies.

II.

Beautiful Homeland, my own dear Homeland,
Prom pine to palm and from glasier to cottonfield;
Great rivers flowing, sweet breezes blowing
O'er Thy vast prairies, Thy forest clad hills.
Fair are those other lands that lure from o'er the sea,
Fair are their maidens who have often smiled on me;
But I shall be true to Thee, oh homeland of mine
And my heart shall evermore your dear earth enshrine.
      Homeland . . . . . Homeland

Repeat refrain.

It is not known when this poem was completed.

This song is taken from a typed manuscript at the Huntington Library with the following note: Lyrics by Jack London; Music by Neil Moret. However, there is no musical score shown.

AND SOME NIGHT

"And some night,
You will find me in your arms,
Pleading—
For the eventual white flame
of your lips!"

It is not known when this poem was completed.

Taken from a manuscript at the Huntington Library.

YOUR KISS

Your kiss, beloved, was to me
As if all flowers of Araby,
And every fresh and fragrant rose
That ever blew, shall blow, or blows
Had all her sweetness taken up
And poured into one perfect cup
For me to drain . . .
Kiss me again!

It is not known when this poem was completed.

Taken from a manuscript at the Huntington Library. A note describes it as a song.

TOO LATE

Too late' Even Is death too late'
    Had it but come—silence' Put out
These sniffling fools that wait,
    With hungry jowl and slobbered snout,
My end—foregathered at the feast
    Like jackals when the lion is dead.
But you, who were among the least
    Of all my friends, stay by my bed.

It is not known when this poem was completed.

It was taken from a manuscript at the Huntington Library.

WHEN ALL THE WORLD SHOUTED MY NAME

When all the world shouted my name,
    Did I remember you, dear friend?
You, who by closest bonds could claim
    My memory? Yes, in the end,
When all the world no longer cried
    My name, but mocked my nakedness,
Spat In my face, and sneered, and lied,
    And damned in very wantoness.

You—why it seems but yesterday,
    We cradled in the self-same nook,
And dreamed, as foolish childhood may,
    Of Life's great game, and undertook
Wild, youthful oaths—swore full and strong,
    To share alike each joy and pain,
To face the utmost, right the wrong,
    Let nothing come between us twain.

And, then—our paths did twist apart.
    You led your uneventful life
In quiet places, played your part
    Softly, took to your breast a wife,
Whose soul was so attuned to yours,
    That hand in hand—nor vain the quest—
You sought, you found the golden shores,
    The Happy Islands of the Blest.

Not so with me: I trod the path
    Of my own choosing—and alone.
Naught could obstruct my course—the wrath
    Of men, the hot curse, nor the moan
Of those who sank beneath my arm,
    Could stay my arm, or ease the blow.
I grasped for greater things—the charm
    Of life like yours I did not know.

A score of phantoms did I chase,
    And when, in turn, each grasped in hand,
I paused a moment from the race,
    Panting, I could not understand—

They were but phantoms, nothing more;
   The time had passed, I could not joy
In what I had so struggled for—
   A bright bauble—a pretty toy.

Success did crown my every effort;
   But herein lay the great mistake—
I, who from all things could extort
   Subservience, did not partake
Of the reward until too late;
   When I at last did grasp the thing
For which I strove, it was my fate
   To find desire had taken wing.

It is not known when this poem was completed.

It was taken from a manuscript at the Huntington Library.

Jack writing on a rowing boat.

Jack London at his desk.

Jack dictating to Charmian

Jack in the office

Jack writing outdoors.

SECTION C

VERSE IN JACK LONDON'S WRITING ATTRIBUTED TO OTHERS

In this section we have gathered all the verse that appears in Jack London's writing, whether fiction or nonfiction, which is attributed to an author other than Jack London. This also includes a number of pieces of verse, where the original author is unknown but have appeared in publications prior to Jack London's use, and they are therefore assumed to have been written by another author.

Each extract will follow the same structure as follows:

1. **Published**: This refers to the first publication in which the verse appears and will be in bold and italicized, omitted when not published. In the case of individual stories, this covers a wide range of publications from magazines to newspapers, periodicals and first edition books. All citings are with volume, chapter and page as appropriate.

2. **Story**: Where applicable this refers to the particular book, story, essay or play in which the verse appears. The story, essay or play will be in quotes plus chapter and page from the first edition book as appropriate in parenthesis.

3. Verses or Song Lyrics as they appear when first published.

4. **Attribution**: Where possible the following information is provided:

    a.   Author of the verse.
    b.   Book (in italics) and poem (in quotes).
    c.   Verses from full poem.
    d.   Any other notes or comments (in parenthesis).

Published: ***The High School Aegis* (October 21, 1895)**
(Volume 10, pages 1-4. This is the paper produced by Oakland High School where Jack London went to school)

Story: "One More Unfortunate"
(This and other stories were collected and published in ***Jack London in the Aegis* (1981)**)

> The sea is still and deep;
> All things within its bosom sleep;
> A single step and all is o'er;
> A plunge, a bubble and no more.

Attribution: **Henry Wadsworth Longfellow** (1807-1882)
Christus: A Mystery, Part II: The Golden Legend, V—A Covered Bridge at Lucerne, "The Inn at Genoa"
Verses 49-52
(This verse also appears in the story, "Devil's Dice Box" and book ***Martin Eden* (1909)** (chapter XXX, page 328))

Story: "Strange Experiences of a Misogynist"
(Written in 1897 and appears on page 55 of ***The Complete Short Stories of Jack London* (1993)**)

> Reuben, Reuben, I've been thinking what a good
> Thing it would be,
> If the women were transported, far beyond the
> Northern sea.

Attribution: **Emma Hart Willard** (1787–1870) (Words) and **Joseph Philip Knight** (1812-1887) (Music)
"Reuben and Rachel" published by C. E. Horn, NY., 1840.
(This extract is an adaptation of a vaudeville song (comic duet), between a woman and a man. The extract should have referred to men rather than women. The original verses are as follows:

> Reuben, I have long been thinking,
> What a good world this might be,
> If the men were all transported
> Far beyond the Northern Sea.
>
> Rachel, I have long been thinking,
> What a fine world this might be,
> If we had some more young ladies
> On this side the Northern Sea.)

Published: *The Owl* **(September 1897)**
             (Volume 3, pages 43-48)

Story: "Two Gold Bricks"
             (Appears in *The Complete Short Stories of Jack London* (1993))

   When some proud son of man returns to earth,
   Unknown to glory but upheld by birth,
   The Sculptor's art exhausts the pomp of woe,
   And storied urns record who sets below;
   When all is done, upon the tomb is seen,
   Not what he was, but what he should have been.

Attribution: **George Gordon Byron [Lord Byron]** (1788-1824).
                 "Boatswain"
                 Verses 1-6
                 (Inscribed on the grave side monument to Byron's pet dog.)

Published: *Outing* **(Albany, N.Y.) (August 1900)**
             (Volume 36, pages 474-477)

Story: "Jan, The Unrepentant"
             (Page 140, appears in *The God of His Fathers* (1901))

   For there's never a law of God or man
   Runs north of Fifty-three.

Attribution: **Rudyard Kipling** (1865-1936)
                 The Seven Seas—"The Rhymes of the Three Sealers"
                 Verse 80.
                 (In the original poem these two verses are one, ending in a colon.)

Published: *Outing* **(December 1900)**
             (Volume 37, pages 276-282)

Story: "Where the Trail Forks"
             (Page 185, collected in *The God of His Fathers* (1901))

Must I, then, must I, then, now leave this town—
And you, my love, stay here?—

Attribution: Schwabian Folk-song but the author is unknown.

Published: *A Daughter of the Snows* **(1902)**
             (Chapter VIII, page 85)

> Bear witness, O my comrades, what a hard-bit gang were we,—
> The servants of the sweep-head, but the masters of the sea!

Attribution: **Rudyard Kipling** (1865-1936)
Departmental Ditties and Other Verses: "The Galley-Slave"
Verses 17-18

Published: *A Daughter of the Snows* (1902)
(Chapter XX, page 210)

> Oh, cable this message along the track;
> The Prod's out West, but he's coming back;
> Put plenty of veal for one on the rack,
> Trolla la la, la la la, la la!

Attribution: **Patrick Sarsfield Gilmore (1829–1892)** (aka: **Louis Lambert**)
The first three verses of the chorus to the song "The Prodigal Son," plus a standard substitute for words.
(The song was printed in *Popular College Songs: A Collection of the Latest Songs as Sung at Harvard and Other Colleges, Together with the Best of the Old Favorites* (1891). The song was set to the music of "When Johnny comes marching home again," also written by **Louis Lambert**.

Published: *A Daughter of the Snows* (1902)
(Chapter IX, page 96-97)

> Truth is within ourselves; it takes no rise
> From outward things, whate'er you may believe.

and

> There is an inmost centre in us all,
> Where truth abides in fulness; and around.

and

> Wall upon wall, the gross flesh hems it in,

Attribution: **Robert Browning** (1812-1889)
"Paracelsus"
Verses 1-2, 3-4 and 5

Published: *The Kempton-Wace Letters* (1903)
        (Title page)

  And of naught else than Love would we discourse.

Attribution: **Dante Alighieri** (1265-1321)
                Dante, Petrarch, Camoens: CXXIV Sonnets, by **Dante Alighieri**, **Francesco Petrarca**, Translated by **Richard Garnett**, (1896)
                "Sonnet II"
                Verse 12
                (In the original the word 'naught' is spelt 'nought' with a colon at the end.)

Published: *The Kempton-Wace Letters* (1903)
        (Chapter III, page 13)

  I made no vows; vows were made for me,
  Bond unknown to me was given
  That I should be, else sinning greatly,
  A dedicated spirit.

Attribution: **William Wordsworth** (1770-1850)
                The Prelude: Book IV—"Summer Vacation"
                Verses 334-337

Published: *The Kempton-Wace Letters* (1903)
        (Chapter III, page 15)

  The Poet, gentle creature that he is,
  Hath, like the Lover, his unruly times;
  His fits when he is neither sick nor well,
  Though no distress be near him but his own
  Unmanageable thoughts.

Attribution: **William Wordsworth** (1770-1850)
                The Prelude: Book I—Introduction—"Childhood and School-time"
                Verses 135-139

Published: *The Kempton-Wace Letters* (1903)
        (Chapter X, page 55)

  Life is worth living
  Through every grain of it,
  From the foundations

> To the last edge
> Of the cornerstone, death.

Attribution: **William Ernest Henley** (1849-1903)
Rhymes and Rhythms: Part XIV—"To J. A. C."
Verses 31-35

Published: *The Kempton-Wace Letters* (1903)
(Chapter XV, page 96)

> Because of our souls' yearning that we meet
> And mix in soul through flesh, which yours and mine
> Wear and impress, and make their visible selves,—
> All which means, for the love of you and me,
> Let us become one flesh, being one soul.

Attribution: **Robert Browning** (1812-1889)
The Ring and the Book: Chapter VII—"Pompilia"
Verses 775-779

Published: *The Kempton-Wace Letters* (1903)
(Chapter XVI, page 107)

> Ah, from what agonies of heart and brain,
> What exultations trampling on despair,
> What tenderness, what tears, what hate of wrong,
> What passionate outcry of a soul in pain,
> Uprose this poem of the earth and air,
> This mediaeval miracle of song!

Attribution: **Henry Wadsworth Longfellow** (1807-1882)
"Divina Commedia," Part II
Verses 23-28

Published: *The Kempton-Wace Letters* (1903)
(Chapter XXX, page 223)

> . . . a fire, smoke . . . no, it's not . . .
> It's vapour done up like a new-born babe—
> (In that shape when you die it leaves your mouth)
> It's . . . well, what matters talking, it's the soul!

Attribution: **Robert Browing** (1812-1889)
"Fra Lippo Lippi"
Verses 185-188

Section C - Poetry in Jack London's Writing Attributed to Others

Published: *The Kempton-Wace Letters* **(1903)**
  (Chapter XXXI, page 254)

  Give all to love;
  Obey thy heart;
  Friends, kindred, days,
  Estate, good fame,
  Plans, credits, and the Muse,—
  Nothing, refuse,

Attribution: **Ralph Emerson** (1803-1882)
  "Give All To Love"
  Verses 1-6

Published: *The Kempton-Wace Letters* **(1903)**
  (Chapter XXXIV, page 235)

  Already how am I so far
  Out of that minute? Must I go
  Still like the thistle-ball, no bar,
  Onward, whenever light wind blows,
  Fixed by no friendly star?

Attribution: **Robert Browning** (1812-1889)
  "Two in the Campagna," Part XI
  Verses 51-55

Published: *The Call of the Wild* **(1903)**
  (Chapter I, page 15)

  Old longings nomadic leap,
  Chafing at custom's chain;
  Again from its brumal sleep
  Wakens the ferine strain.

Attribution: **John Myers O'Hara** (1870-1944)
  "Atavism"
  Verses 1-4

Published: *The People of the Abyss* **(1903)**
  (After title page)

  O Lord and Master, not ours the guilt,
  We build but as our fathers built;

Behold thine images how they stand
Sovereign and sole through all our land.

Our task is hard—with sword and flame,
To hold thine earth forever the same.
And with sharp crooks of steel to keep,
Still as thou leftest them, they sheep.

Then Christ sought out an artisan,
A low-browed, stunted, haggard man,
And a motherless girl whose fingers thin
Crushed from her faintly want and sin.

These set he in the midst of them,
And as they drew back their garment hem
For fear of defilement, "Lo, here," said he,
"The images ye have made of me."

Attribution:	**James Russell Lowell** (1819-1891)
	The poetical works of James Russell Lowell, "A Parable"
	Verses 33-44

Published:	*The People of the Abyss* **(1903)**
	(Chapter I - The Descent, page 1)

Christ look upon us in this city,
And keep our sympathy and pity
Fresh, and our faces heavenward;
Lest we grow hard.

Attribution:	**Thomas Ashe** (1836-1889)
	"London Lyrics," (1.) I—PROLOGUE
	Verses 1-4

Published:	*The People of the Abyss* **(1903)**
	(Chapter III – My Lodging and Some Others, page 23)

The poor, the poor, the poor, they stand,
Wedged by the pressing of Trade's hand,
Against an inward-opening door
That pressure tightens evermore;
They sigh a monstrous, foul-air sigh
For the outside leagues of liberty,

> Where art, sweet lark, translates the sky
> Into a heavenly melody.

Attribution: **Sidney Lanier** (1842-1881)
"The Symphony"
Verses 21-28

Published: *The People of the Abyss* (1903)
(Chapter IV – A Man and the Abyss, page 30)

> After a momentary silence spake
> Some vessel of a more ungainly make;
> They sneer at me for leaning all awry:
> What! did the hand then of the Potter shake?

Attribution: **Omar Khayyam** (1048-1131)
"Rubaiyat"
Quatrain LXXXVI (86)

Published: *The People of the Abyss* (1903)
(Chapter VI – Frying-Pan Alley and a Glimpse of Inferno, page 54)

> The beasts they hunger, and eat, and die,
> And so do we, and the world's a sty.
> "Swinehood hath no remedy,"
> Say many men, and hasten by.

Attribution: **Sidney Lanier** (1842-1881)
"Symphony"
Verses 35-36 & 38-39
(Jack London altered the original:
  i. Verse 35 a comma was omitted after 'beasts' and the end comma replaces an original semi-colon.
  ii. Verse 36 the full stop replaces an original semi-colon.
  iii. Verse 37, from the original poem, was left out of this extract.
  iv. Verse 39 the full stop replaces an original comma.)

Published: *The People of the Abyss* (1903)
(Chapter VII – A Winner of the Victoria Cross, page 67)

> By the brand upon my shoulder, by the gall of clinging steel;
> By the welt the whips have left me, by the scars that never heal;
> By eyes grown old with staring through the sun-wash on the brine,
> I am paid in full for service. . .

Attribution: **Rudyard Kipling** (1865-1936)

"The Galley-Slave"
Verses 29-32
(Jack London altered the original:
  i. Verse 26 a hyphen added between "sun" and "wash."
  ii. Verse 32 has been shortened from the original.
  Verses 29 & 30 also appear in Chapter 35 of ***Mutiny of the Elsinore*** **(1914).**)

Published: ***The People of the Abyss*** **(1903)**
(Chapter XII - Coronation Day, page 138)

O thou that sea-walls sever
From lands unwalled by seas!
Wilt thou endure forever,
O Milton's England, these?
Thou that wast his Republic,
Wilt thou clasp their knees?
These royalties rust-eaten,
These worm-corroded lies
That keep thy head storm-beaten,
And sun-like strength of eyes
From the open air and heaven
Of intercepted skies!

Attribution: **Algernon Charles Swinburne** (1837-1909)
"A Marching Song"
Verses 86-95
(Jack London altered the original by:
  i. Changing the first word of verse 86 from "And" to "O."
  ii. Splitting verses 90 (5 & 6 of extract) and 95 (11 & 12 of extract) from one into two separate verses.
  iii. Joining the original quintain's into one continuous poem.)

Published: ***The People of the Abyss*** **(1903)**
(Chapter XII - Coronation Day, page 147)

Oh! on Coronation Day, on Coronation Day,
We'll have a spree, a jubilee, and shout, Hip, hip, hooray,
For we'll all be merry, drinking whiskey, wine, and sherry,
We'll be merry on Coronation Day.

Attribution: (Unknown author of a traditional English (London) street song.)

Published: ***The People of the Abyss*** **(1903)**
(Chapter XII - Coronation Day, page 148)

Section C - Poetry in Jack London's Writing Attributed to Others

> Yew aw the enny, ennyseckle, Oi em ther bee,
> Oi'd like ter sip ther enny from those red lips, yew see.

Attribution: Unknown author of a traditional English (London) street song "The Honeysuckle and the Bee."

Published: *The People of the Abyss* (1903)
    (Chapter XIII – Dan Cullen, Docker, page 158)

> Life scarce can tread majestically
> Foul court and fever-stricken alley.

Attribution: **Thomas Ashe** (1836-1889)
    "London Lyrics," (1.) I—PROLOGUE
    Verses 9-10

Published: *The People of the Abyss* (1903)
    (Chapter XIV - Hops and Hoppers, page 167)

> Ill fares the land, to hastening ills a prey,
> Where wealth accumulates and men decay:
> Princes and Lords may flourish, or may fade;
> A breath can make them, as a breath is made;
> But a bold peasantry, their country's pride,
> When once destroyed, can never be supplied.

Attribution: **Oliver Goldsmith** (1730–1774),
    "The Deserted Village"
    Verses 51-56
    (Jack London altered the punctuation from the original:
        i. Verse 52 the end colon replaces a full stop in the original.
        ii. Verse 53 the end semi-colon replaces a comma in the original
        iii. Verse 55 the hyphen between "peasantry-country" and at the end of the verse are omitted from the original.)

Published: *The People of the Abyss* (1903)
    (Chapter XV - The Sea Wife, page 183)

> There dwells a wife by the Northern Gate,
> And a wealthy wife is she;
> She breeds a breed o' rovin' men
> And casts them over sea.
>
> And some are drowned in deep water,
> And some in sight of shore;

And word goes back to the weary wife,
And ever she sends more.

Attribution: **Rudyard Kipling** (1865-1936)
               "Sea-Wife"
               Verses 1-8

Published: *The People of the Abyss* **(1903)**
           (Chapter XVIII — Wages, page 202)

Some sell their lives for bread;
Some sell their souls for gold;
Some seek the river bed;
Some seek the workhouse mould.

Such is proud England's sway,
Where wealth may work its will;
White flesh is cheap to-day,
White souls are cheaper still.

Attribution: **Fantasias**
               (This attribution was written by Jack London. However, this is
               unlikely to be the name of the author but could be the title of the
               poem. These two stanzas appear in *Merrie England – A plain
               exposition of Socialism* by **Robert Blatchford** (Pub. 1895),
               widely circulated at the time.)

Published: *The People of the Abyss* **(1903)**
           (Chapter XIX – The Ghetto, page 210)

Is it well that while we range with Science, glorying in the time,
City children soak and blacken soul and sense in city slime?
There among the gloomy alleys Progress halts on palsied feet;
Crime and hunger cast out maidens by the thousand on the
                                                    street;

There the master scrimps his haggard seamstress of her
                                                    daily bread;
There the single sordid attic holds the living and the dead;
There the smouldering fire of fever creeps across the
                                                    rotted floor,
And the crowded couch of incest, in the warrens of the poor.

Section C - Poetry in Jack London's Writing Attributed to Others

Attribution: **Alfred Lord Tennyson** (1809-1892)
"Locksley Hall Sixty Years After"
Verses 215-222

Published: *The People of the Abyss* **(1903)**
(Chapter XXIII — The Children, page 274)

> Where home is a hovel, and dull we grovel,
> Forgetting the world is fair.

Attribution: **William Morris** (1834-1896)
"Chants for Socialist"
Verses 17-18

Published: *The People of the Abyss* **(1903)**
(Chapter XXIII — The Children, page 277)

> Dull despair and misery
> Lie about them from their birth;
> Ugly curses, uglier mirth,
> Are their earliest lullaby.

Attribution: **Mathlide Blind** (1841-1896)
"The Street-Children's Dance"
Verses 49-52

Published: *The People of the Abyss* **(1903)**
(Chapter XXVIII – The Management, pages 318-319

CHALLENGE

> I have a vague remembrance
> Of a story that is told
> In some ancient Spanish legend
> Or chronicle of old.
>
> It was when brave King Sanche
> Was before Zamora slain,
> And his great besieging army
> Lay encamped upon the plain.
>
> Don Diego de Ordenez
> Sallied forth in front of all,
> And shouted loud his challenge
> To the warders on the wall.

All the people of Zamora,
Both the born and the unborn,
As traitors did he challenge
With taunting words of scorn.

The living in their houses,
And in their graves the dead,
And the waters in their rivers,
And their wine, and oil, and bread.

There is a greater army
That besets us round with strife,
A starving, numberless army
At all the gates of life.

The poverty-stricken millions
Who challenge our wine and bread,
And impeach us all as traitors,
Both the living and the dead.

And whenever I sit at the banquet,
Where the feast and song are high,
Amid the mirth and music
I can hear that fearful cry.

And hollow and haggard faces
Look into the lighted hall,
And wasted hands are extended
To catch the crumbs that fall

And within there is light and plenty,
And odours fill the air;
But without there is cold and darkness,
And hunger and despair.

And there in the camp of famine,
In wind, and cold, and rain,
Christ, the great Lord of the Army,
Lies dead upon the plain.

Attribution: **Henry Longfellow** (1807-1882)
Birds of Passage: Flight the Third: "The Challenge"
Entire poem.

Section C - Poetry in Jack London's Writing Attributed to Others

Published: ***Sunset Magazine* (June 1903)**
(Volume 11, 103a, pages 114-121)

Story: "The Faith of Men"
(Page 73, appears in *The Faith of Men and Other Stories* **(1904)**)

> Hear me babble what the weakest won't confess—
> I am Memory and Torment—I am Town!
> I am all that ever went with evening dress!

Attribution: **Rudyard Kipling** (1865-1936)
"Song of the Banjo"
Verses 30-32

Published: ***Sunset Magazine* (June 1903)**
(Volume 11, 103a, pages 114-121)

Story: "The Faith of Men"
(Page 74, appears in *The Faith of Men and Other Stories* **(1904)**)

> The flocks are folded, boughs are bare,
> The salmon takes the sea;
> And oh, my fair, would I somewhere
> Might house my heart with thee.

Attribution: **John Vance Cheney** (1848-1922)
"Somewhere"
Verses 5-8

Published: *Ainslee's* **(October 1903)**
(Volume 12, pages 74-82)

Story: "Local Color"
(Page 28, appears in *Moon Face and Other Stories* **(1906)**)

> The case of a treble hautboy
> Was a mansion for him, a court.

Attribution: **William Shakespeare** (1564-1616)
"Henry IV," Part II, Act III, scene ii (Original version)
Verses 284-285

Published: *The Sea-Wolf* **(1904)**
(Chapter VII, pages 72-73)

O the blazing tropic night, when the wake's a welt of light
That holds the hot sky tame,
And the steady forefoot snores through the planet-powdered floors
Where the scared whale flukes in flame!
Her plates are scarred by the sun, dear lass,
And her ropes are taut with the dew,
For we're booming down on the old trail, our own trail, the out trail,
We're sagging south on the Long Trail—the trail that is always new.

Attribution: **Rudyard Kipling** (1865-1936)
"L'Envoi"
Verses 56-63

Published: *The Sea-Wolf* **(1904)**
(Chapter XI, page 108)

What, without asking, hither hurried *Whence*?
And, without asking, *Whither* hurried hence!
Oh, many a Cup of this forbidden Wine
Must drown the memory of that insolence!

Attribution: **Omar Khayyam** (1048-1131)
"Rubaiyat" (1879 Translation by **Edward FitzGerald**)
Quatrain XXX (30)
(This quatrain was also used in the essay "Fomá Gordyéeff" in the book ***Revolution and Other Essays* (1910)**.)

Published: *The Sea-Wolf* **(1904)**
(Chapter XXIII, page 216)

I wandered all these years among
A world of women, seeking you.

Attribution: **Arthur William Symons** (1865-1945)
London Nights (Pub. 1895), "Magnificat"
Verses 6-7

Published: *The Sea-Wolf* **(1904)**
(Chapter VII, page 74)

Oh, I am the wind the seamen love—
I am steady, and strong, and true;
They follow my track by the clouds above,
O'er the fathomless tropic blue.

Through daylight and dark I follow the bark,
I keep like a hound on her trail;
I'm strongest at noon, yet under the moon,
I stiffen the bunt of her sail.

Attribution: **Thomas Fleming Day** (1861-1927)
"The Trade-Wind's Song" Publishing in *Sailor's Magazine*, page 98, Vol 72, April, 1900.
Verses 1-4 and 25-28
(Jack London refers to it as the "Song of the Trade Wind" in the narrative. He has altered the poem:
i. Verse 1 the word "that" is added before "the."
ii. Verse 1 removed the comma at the end and replace it with an emdash.
iii. Verse 2 commas added after "steady" and "strong."
iv. Verse 3 the end comma removed.
v. Verse 4 removed a comma after "fathomless."
Verses 7 & 8 also appears in Chapter XXVII, page 237, of *Martin Eden*.)

Published: *The Sea-Wolf* (1904)
(Chapter XXIII, page 216)

I lived with visions for my company
Instead of men and women years ago,
And found them gentle mates, nor thought to know
A sweeter music than they played to me.

Attribution: **Elizabeth Barrett Browning** (1806-1861)
"Sonnets from the Portuguese"
Part XXVI, Verses 1-4

Published: *The Sea-Wolf* (1904)
(Chapter XXVI, page 246)

Blessed am I beyond women even herein,
That beyond all born women is my sin,
And perfect my transgression.

Attribution: **Algernon Charles Swinburne** (1837-1909)
Tristram of Lyonesse: and other poems (1892), "Tristram of Lyonesse: V – Iseult at Tintagel"
Verses 2271-2273
(Jack London has altered the following:
i. Verse 2271 first word changed from "Blest" to "Blessed."
ii. Verse 2273 shortened and colon replaced with a full-stop.)

Published: ***The Sea-Wolf* (1904)**
          (Chapter XXVI, page 248)

> And her eyes should be my light while the sun went out behind me,
> And viols in her voice be the last sound in mine ear.

Attribution: **Ernest Dowson** (1867-1900)
                  "Impenitentia Ultima"
                  Verses: 29-32

Published: ***The Sea-Wolf* (1904)**
          (Chapter XXVI, page 249)

> … … … …Here at least
> We shall be free; the Almighty hath not built
> Here for his envy; will not drive us hence;
> Here we may reign secure; and in my choice
> To reign is worth ambition, though in hell:
> Better to reign in hell than serve in heaven.

Attribution: **John Milton** (1667-1674)
                  "Paradise Lost:" Book I
                  Verses 258-263 (1674 Version)

Published: ***The Youth's Companion* (March 17, 1904)**
          (Volume 78, pages 129-130)

Story: "The Banks of the Sacramento"
                (Page 52, appears in ***Dutch Courage* (1922)**)

> Chorus:
> And it's blow, ye winds, heigh-ho,
> For Cal-i-for-ni-o;
> For there's plenty of gold so I've been told,
> On the banks of the Sacramento!

Attribution: **Frank Shay** (1888-1954)
                  "Iron Men & Wooden Ships," (Song)
                (The first stanza is slightly altered from the original. There is some speculation as to whether it was created by the Hutchinson Family who popularized the song and subsequently published the text in their 1855 song book.)

Section C - Poetry in Jack London's Writing Attributed to Others

Published: ***The Century Magazine*** **(November 1905)**
(Volume 71, pages 117-127)

Story: "All Gold Canyon"
(Page 153, appears in ***Moon-Face and Other Stories*** **(1906)**)

> Tu'n around an' tu'n yo' face
> Untoe them sweet hills of grace
> (D' pow'rs of sin yo' am scornin'!).
> Look about an' look aroun',
> Fling yo' sin–pack on d' groun'
> (Yo' will meet wid d' Lord in d' mornin'!).

Attribution: **Alfred Henry Lewis** (1855-1914)
Wolfville Days (1902)
Page 294.
(Jack London altered the poem:
  i. Verse 1 omitted comma from end.
  ii. Verse 2 replaced "o'" with "of."
  iii. Verse 3 made "s" of "sin" lower case.
  iv. Verse 4 replaced "a oun'," with "aroun'."
  v. Verse 5 removed full stop from end of verse.
  vi. Verse 6 replaced a full stop at end of verse with an explanation mark.)

Published: ***McClure's Magazine*** **(December 1905)**
(Volume 26, pages 144-158)
Blackwood's Magazine **(Edinburgh), (December 1905)**
(Volume 178, pages 765-780)

Story: "Love of Life"
(Page 3, appears in ***Love of Life & Other Stories*** **(1907)**)

> This out of all will remain—
> They have lived and have tossed:
> So much of the game will be gain,
> Though the gold of the dice has been lost.

Attribution: **Hamlin Hannibal Garland** (1860-1940)
The Trail of the Gold Seekers: A Record of Travel in Prose and Verse. (Pub. 1899), "The Gold-Seekers."
Verses 29-32
(Jack London altered the poem:
  i. Verse 1 the first word "But" is omitted.
  ii. Verse 1 end of the verse the comma replaced with a emdash.
  iii. Verse 2 end of the verse the semi-colon is replaced by a colon.)

Published: ***Woman's Home Companion* (September 1906)**
              (Volume 33, pages 5-7 and 49)

Story: "The Apostate"
              (Page 27, appears in *When God Laughs and Other Stories* **(1911)**)

> Now I wake me up to work;
> I pray the Lord I may not shirk.
> If I should die before the night,
> I pray the Lord my work's all right.
> Amen

Attribution: **Thomas Osborne Davis** (1814-1845)
              (Jack London probably adapted his prayer from this version:
              > Now I get me up to work,
              > I pray the Lord I may not shirk;
              > And if I die before tonight,
              > I pray my work will be all right.

Published: ***The Smart Set* (January 1907)**
              (Volume 21, pages 39-44)

Story: "When God Laughs"
              (Page 3, appears in *When God Laughs and Other Stories* **(1911)**)

> The gods, the gods are stronger; time
> Falls down before them, all men's knees
> Bow, all men's prayers and sorrows climb
> Like incense toward them; yea, for these
> Are gods, Felise."

Attribution: **Algernon Charles Swinburne** (1837-1909)
              "Felise"
              Verses 186-190

Published: ***The Smart Set* (January 1907)**
              (Volume 21, pages 39-44)

Story: "When God Laughs"
              (Page 15, appears in *When God Laughs and Other Stories* **(1911)**)

> And time could only tutor us to eke
> Our rapture's warmth with custom's afterglow.

also

Kiss we and part; no further can we go;
And better death than we from high to low
Should dwindle, or decline from strong to weak.

Attribution: **Alfred Austin** (1835-1913)
"Love's Wisdom"
Verses 7-8 & 2-4

Published: *The Smart Set* **(January 1907)**
(Volume 21, pages 39-44)

Story: "When God Laughs"
(Chapter I, page 19, appears in ***When God Laughs and Other Stories* (1911)**)

Love's Waiting Time *(Title of the poem in the narrative preceding these verses)*

So sweet it is to stand but just apart,
To know each other better, and to keep
The soft, delicious sense of two that touch . . .

O love, not yet! . . . Sweet, let us keep our love
Wrapped round with sacred mystery awhile,
Waiting the secret of the coming years,
That come not yet, not yet . . . sometime . . . not yet . . .
Oh, yet a little while our love may grow!
When it has blossomed it will haply die.
Feed it with lipless kisses, let it sleep,
Bedded in dead denial yet some while . . .
Oh, yet a little while, a little while.

Attribution: **Curtis Hidden Page** (1870-1946)
"Love's Waiting-Time"
Verses 10-12, 1-4, and 5-9.
(Jack London rearranged the stanzas by placed the first three verses of the third stanza first, followed by stanza one and two. He further altered the poem:
  i. Removed the dash joining "Waiting-Room" from title.
  ii. First three verses of stanza three placed first, as if the first stanza.
  iii. Verse 3 removed a comma before the ellipse.
  iv. Verse 9 removed the ellipse.
  v. Verse 12 replaced explanation mark with full stop.)

Published: *The Smart Set* **(January 1907)**
             (Volume 21, pages 39-44)

Story: "When God Laughs"
             (Page 24, appears in *When God Laughs and Other Stories* **(1911)**)

> There was not a single hour
> We might have kissed and did not kiss.

Attribution: **Edith Nesbit Bland** (1858-1924)
               Songs of Love and Empire: "Love well the hour"
               Verses 15-16
               (Jack London adapted the original poem verse 15:
                   "The thought that there was ever an hour."
               Jack London may have also adapted a version which appears in
               The Home Book of Verse (American and English 1580-1918)
               edited by **Burton Egbert Stevenson** (Pub. 1912). Here the poem,
               slightly altered from the original, appears with the title "Heart of
               my Heart" but author "Unknown." Interestingly, verse 15 is
               similar to Jack's: "That there was not a single hour.")

Published: *The Road* **(1907)**
             (After the title page)

> Speakin' in general, I 'ave tried 'em all,
> The 'appy roads that take you o'er the world.
> Speakin' in general, I 'ave found them good
> For such as cannot use one bed too long,
> But must get 'ence, the same as I 'ave done,
> An' go observin' matters till they die.

Attribution: **Rudyard Kipling** (1865-1936)
               The Seven Seas, "Sestina of the Tramp-Royal"
               Verses 1-6

Published: *The Road* (1907)
             (Page 53)

> What do it matter where or 'ow we die,
> So long as we've our 'ealth to watch it all—

Attribution: **Rudyard Kipling** (1865-1936)
               The Seven Seas, "Sestina of the Tramp-Royal"
               Verses 7-8

Published: *The Iron heel* **(1908)**
   (Title Page)

At first, this Earth, a stage so gloomed with woe
You almost sicken at the shifting of the scenes.
And yet be patient. Our Playwright may show
In some fifth act what this Wild Drama means.

Attribution: **Lord Alfred Tennyson** (1809-1892)
   Demeter, and other Poems, "The Play"
   Entire poem
   (Jack London altered the poem as follows:
      i. Verse 1 first word altered from "Act" to "At."
      ii. Verse 1 word "gloom'd" changed to "gloomed."
      iii. Verse 2 phrase, "You all but sicken" changed to: "You almost sicken."
      iv. Verse 2 "shifting scenes" changed to "shifting of the scenes."
      v. Verse 4 words "act" changed to "Act" and "wild" to "Wild.")

Published: *The Iron heel* **(1908)**
   (Page 115)

The silver trumpets rang across the Dome;
The people knelt upon the ground with awe:
And borne upon the necks of men I saw,
Like some great God, the Holy Lord of Rome.
Priest-like, he wore a robe more white than foam,
And, king-like, swathed himself in royal red,
Three crowns of gold rose high upon his head:
In splendor and in light the Pope passed home.

My heart stole back across wide wastes of years
To One who wandered by a lonely sea,
And sought in vain for any place of rest:
"Foxes have holes, and every bird its nest,
I, only I, must wander wearily,
And bruise my feet, and drink wine salt with tears.

Attribution: **Oscar Wilde** (1854-1900)
   Rosa Mystica: "Easter Day"
   Verses: entire poem

Published: ***The Iron heel* (1908)**
    (Chapter XI – The Great Adventure, pages 184-186)

    Joy upon joy and gain upon gain
    Are the destined rights of my birth,
    And I shout the praise of my endless days
    To the echoing edge of the earth.
    Though I suffer all deaths that a man can die
    To the uttermost end of time,
    I have deep-drained this, my cup of bliss,
    In every age and clime—
    The froth of Pride, the tang of Power,
    The sweet of Womanhood!
    I drain the lees upon my knees,
    For oh, the draught is good;
    I drink to Life, I drink to Death,
    And smack my lips with song,
    For when I die, another 'I' shall pass the cup along.

    The man you drove from Eden's grove
        Was I, my Lord, was I,
    And I shall be there when the earth and the air
        Are rent from sea to sky;
    For it is my world, my gorgeous world,
        The world of my dearest woes,
    From the first faint cry of the newborn
        To the rack of the woman's throes.

    Packed with the pulse of an unborn race,
    Torn with a world's desire,
    The surging flood of my wild young blood
    Would quench the judgment fire.
    I am Man, Man, Man, from the tingling flesh
    To the dust of my earthly goal,
    From the nestling gloom of the pregnant womb
    To the sheen of my naked soul.
    Bone of my bone and flesh of my flesh
    The whole world leaps to my will,
    And the unslaked thirst of an Eden cursed
    Shall harrow the earth for its fill.
    Almighty God, when I drain life's glass
    Of all its rainbow gleams,
    The hapless plight of eternal night

Shall be none too long for my dreams.

The man you drove from Eden's grove
    Was I, my Lord, was I,
And I shall be there when the earth and the air
    Are rent from sea to sky;
For it is my world, my gorgeous world,
    The world of my dear delight,
From the brightest gleam of the Arctic stream
    To the dusk of my own love-night.

Attribution: **Eleanor Hallowell Abbott** (1809-1892)
Harpers Magazine (Pub. 1902, Vol. CV, June to November 1902, pages 144 - 145)
"The Song of the Man"
Jack London's 4 stanzas are the 5, 6, 3, and 2 of the original, verses 49 to 64, 65 to 72, 25 to 40, and 17 to 24.
This original poem has a structure of 8 stanzas, which are organized as four sets of 16 and then 8 verse stanzas. Jack London selected 4 stanzas in sets but not in the same order as the original.
(Jack London further altered the poem as follows:

    i.   Verse 7 the word "the" altered to "my."
    ii.   Verse 7 the word "cup" and "bliss" changed from initial capitals.
    iii.   Verse 8 end full stop replaced with a hyphen.
    iv.   Verse 9 words "Pride" and "Power" changed from regular type.
    v.   Verse 10 the end comma followed by a dash is replaced by an explanation mark.
    vi.   Verse 12 a full stop is replaced with a semi-colon.
    vii.   Verse 15 two verses joined together also with a comma after "die" and half quotes around the word "I."
    viii.   Verse 19 the end semi-colon replaces a full stop.
    ix.   Verse 22 the dash in "new-born" removed and the last word "I" removed.
    x.   Verse 25 the initial capital letter of "world's" turned to regular.
    xi.   Verse 27 the initial capital letter of "judgment" turned to regular.
    xii.   Verse 28 phrase "man, *man*, MAN" replaced with "Man, Man, Man,"
    xiii.   Verse 32 end full stop removed.
    xiv.   Verse 33 end full stop replaced with comma.
    xv.   Verse 35 word "harry" replaced with "harrow."
    xvi.   Verse 36 makes verse one sentence by replacing explanation after "God!" with comma and removes the initial capital from "When" with regular.
    xvii.   Verse 39 replaced first word "Would" with "Shall" and replaced explanation mark at end with full stop.

Published: ***Lady's Realm* (London), (December 1908)**
             (Volume 25, pages 170-175)

Story: "Aloha, Oe"
             (Page 134, appears in ***The House of Pride* (1912)**)

>   Ka halia ko aloha kai hiki mai,
>   Ke hone ae nei i ku'u manawa,
>   O oe nō ka'u aloha
>   A loko e hana nei.

Attribution: **Lili'uokalani** (Last Monarch of Hawaii)
             "Aloha 'Oe" (Song)
             Second stanza
             (Jack London's version differs slightly from the original but it is essentially the same.)

Published: ***Lady's Realm* (London), (December 1908)**
             (Volume 25, pages 170-175)

Story: "Aloha, Oe"
             (Page 145, appears in ***The House of Pride* (1912)**)

>   **My love to you.**
>   **My love be with you till we meet again.**

Attribution: **Lili'uokalani** (Last Monarch of Hawaii)
             "Aloha 'Oe" (Song)
             Verse 1 (Chorus)
             (Jack London's version differs slightly from the original but it is practically the same.)

Published: ***Lady's Realm* (London), (December 1908)**
             (Volume 25, pages 170-175)

Story: "Aloha, Oe"
             (Page 147, appears in ***The House of Pride* (1912)**)

>   Aloha oe, Aloha oe, e ke onaona no ho ika lipo,
>   A fond embrace, ahoi ae au, until we meet again.

Attribution: **Lili'uokalani** (Last Monarch of Hawaii)
             "Aloha 'Oe" (Song)
             Chorus
             (Jack London's version differs slightly from the original by mixing the English and Hawaiian but it is essentially the same.)

Published: *Martin Eden* **(1909)**
  (After title page)

> Let me live my years in heat of blood!
> Let me lie drunken with the dreamer's wine!
> Let me not see this soul–house built of mud
> Go toppling to the dust of a vacant shrine!

Attribution: **John Gneisenau Neihardt** (1881-1973)
  A Bundle of Myrrh (Pub. 1907), "Let me live my years"
  Verses 1-4
  (Jack London altered the poem as follows:
   i. Verse 4: omitted the emdash between "dust" and "a," and replaced with a hyphen.).

Published: *Martin Eden* **(1909)**
  (Chapter XL, page 344)

> I have done—
> Put by the lute.
> Song and singing soon are over
> As the airy shades that hover
> In among the purple clover.
> I have done—
> Put by the lute.
> Once I sang as early thrushes
> Sing among the dewy bushes;
> Now I'm mute.
> I am like a weary linnet,
> For my throat has no song in it;
> I have had my singing minute.
> I have done.
> Put by the lute.

Attribution: **Duncan Campbell Scott** (1862-1947)
  The Magic House and Other Poems, (Pub. 1893), "Song"
  Entire poem
  (Jack London altered the original poem as follows:
   i. Verse 1 comma omitted and emdash inserted.
   ii. Verse 2 semi-colon replaced with a full stop at end of verse.
   iii. Verse 3 comma omitted from end of verse.
   iv. Verse 4 words "Up above" replaced with "In among" and dash replaced with a full stop.
   v. Verse 6 split into two with emdash inserted. Original verse is: "I have done, put but the lute."

vi.   Verse 8 comma replaced with semi-colon at end of verse.
vii.   Verse 9: replaced semi-colon with full stop at end of verse.
viii.   Verse 11 comma replaced with semi-colon at end of verse.
ix.   Verse 13 comma replaced with full stop.

Published: *Martin Eden* **(1909)**
(Chapter XXXI, page 281)

> Under the bludgeoning of Chance
> My head is bloody but unbowed.

Attribution: **William Ernest Henley** (1849-1903)
"Invictus"
Verses 5-6

Published: *Martin Eden* **(1909)**
(Chapter XLVI, page 409)

> From too much love of living,
> From hope and fear set free,
> We thank with brief thanksgiving
> Whatever gods may be
> That no life lives forever;
> That dead men rise up never;
> That even the weariest river
> Winds somewhere safe to sea.

Attribution: **Algernon Charles Swinburne** (1837-1909)
"The Garden of Prosperine"
Verses 81-88

Published: *The Red Book Magazine* **(Chicago), (June 1909)**
(Volume 13, pages 225-240)

Story: "Good-bye Jack"
(Page 97, appears in *The House of Pride* **(1912)**)

> Thy life is music—Fate the notes prolong!
> Each isle a stanza, and the whole a song.

Attribution: **George. H. Stewart** (1875-1948)
"Hawaii nei"
Verses 5-6
(The original poem appears in *A Trip to Hawaii* (Pub. 1892)

by **Charles Warren Stoddard**, page 20. However, this may not be the full version because the title is omitted. Jack London most probably saw the verses in the *Western Field* by Olympic Club, published 10 years later, which mistakenly refers to **Stoddard** as the author. London repeated this attribution in his narrative and incorrectly spells the title, "Hawaii noi" instead of "Hawaii nei.")

Published: *The Red Book Magazine* **(Chicago), (June 1909)**
(Volume 13, pages 225-240)

Story: "Good-bye Jack"
(Page 116, appears in *The House of Pride* (1912))

> The poor old tramp explains his poor old ulcers;
> Life is, I think, a blunder and a shame.

Attribution: **William Ernest Henley** (1849-1903)
"In Hospital" II – Waiting
Verses 25-26
(Jack London has altered the punctuation from the original:
  i. Verse 1 the full stop is replaced with a semi-colon.
  ii. Verse 2 parenthesis around "I think" is replaced with commas.

Published: *Revolution and Other Essays* **(1910)**

Essay: "Revolution"
(Page ix)

> The present is enough for common souls,
> Who, never looking forward, are indeed
> Mere clay, wherein the footprints of their age
> Are petrified for ever.—

Attribution: **James Russell Lowell** (1819-1891)
"A Glance behind the Curtain"
Verses 244-247

Published: *Revolution and Other Essays* **(1910)**

Essay: "The Somnambulists"
(Page 41)

> 'Tis only fools speak evil of the clay—
> The very stars are made of clay like mine.

Attribution: **Richard Le Gallienne** (1866-1947)
Rubáiyát of Omar Khayyám: A Paraphrase from Several Literal Translations (Published 1897)
Verses 3-4, (First quatrain of four on page 77)
(**Le Gallienne** added 50 quatrains to the original 101 written by **Edward FitzGerald** who had discarded many he thought not worthy of inclusion. Jack London replaced the comma in verse 3 with an emdash.)

Published: *Revolution and Other Essays* **(1910)**

Essay: "The Gold hunters of the North"
(Page 179)

> Where the Northern Lights come down o' nights to dance on the houseless snow.

Attribution: **Rudyard Kipling** (1865-1936)
The Writings in Prose and Verse of Rudyard Kipling (Pub. 1899)
"The Rhyme of the Three Sealers"
Verses 33-34
(Jack London replaces the first word "And" with "Where" and replaces the semi-colon with a full-stop at the end of verse 34.)

Published: *Revolution and Other Essays* **(1910)**

Essay: "These Bones Shall Rise Again"
(Page 229)

> Keep ye the Law—be swift in all obedience.
> Clear the land of evil, drive the road and bridge the ford.
> Make ye sure to each his own
> That he reap what he hath sown;
> By the peace among Our peoples let men know we serve the Lord.

Attribution: **Rudyard Kipling** (1865-1936)
"A Song of the English"
Verses 16-20

Published: *Burning Daylight* **(1910)**
(After title page)

> Man is made *with such large discourse, looking before and after.*

Attribution: **William Shakespeare** (1564-1616)

Words in italics taken from "Hamlet" Act IV, Scene IV
Verses 38-39

Published: *Forum* **(January 1911)**

Story: "The Human Drift"
(Page 1, appears in *The Human Drift* **(1917)**)

The Revelations of Devout and Learn'd
Who rose before us, and as Prophets Burn'd,
Are all but stories, which, awoke from Sleep,
They told their comrades, and to Sleep return'd.

Attribution: **Omar Khayyam** (1048-1131)
"Rubaiyat" (1879 Translation by **Edward FitzGerald**)
Quatrain LXV (65)

Published: *Forum* **(January 1911)**

Story: "The Human Drift"
(Page 7, appears in *The Human Drift* **(1917)**)

The Sword Singing—
Driving the darkness,
Even as the banners
And spears of the Morning;
Sifting the nations,
The Slag from the metal,
The waste and the weak
From the fit and the strong;
Fighting the brute,
The abysmal Fecundity;
Checking the gross
Multitudinous blunders,
The groping, the purblind
Excesses in service
Of the Womb universal,
The absolute drudge.

Attribution: **William Ernest Henley** (1849-1903)
The Song of the Sward and other verse: "The Song of the Sword"
Verses 1-2 and 124-138
(This first verse of this extract is in fact the first two verses of the original poem)

Published: *Forum* **(January 1911)**

Story: "The Human Drift"
(Page 20, appears in *The Human Drift* (1917))

    Follow, O follow, then,
    Heroes, my harvesters!
    Where the tall grain is ripe
    Thrust in your sickles!
    Stripped and adust
    In a stubble of empire
    Scything and binding
    The full sheaves of sovranty.

Attribution: **William Ernest Henley** (1849-1903)
The Song of the Sward and other verse: "The Song of the Sword"
Verses 100-107

Published: *Adventure* **(1911)**
(After title page)

    We are those fools who could not rest
    In the dull earth we left behind,
    But burned with passion for the West,
    And drank strange frenzy from its wind.
    The world where wise men live at ease
    Fades from our unregretful eyes,
    And blind across uncharted seas
    We stagger on our enterprise.

THE SHIP OF FOOLS

Attribution: This stanza is obviously based on the famous *The Ship of Fools* (*Das Narrenschiff*) allegorical poem written by **Sebastian Brandt** in 1492, translated by **Alexander Barclay** into English in 1509. Jack London may have found this verse, adapted by **Sir Ernest Shackleton** (British Antarctic Explorer) from another source, from newspaper reports or his books. Original author unknown.

Published: *The Century Magazine* **(June 1911)**

Play: "The First Poet"
(Page 176, appears in *The Turtles of Tasman* (1916))

> The bright day is gone.
> The night maketh me sa—sad.
> But the stars are very white.
> They whisper that the day shall return.
> O stars; little pieces of the day!

Attribution: **George Sterling** (1869-1926)
(These verses are the poetic centerpiece of "The First Poet" published by Jack London (although written by **George Sterling**). In section F, of this book, the play is reproduced in full and details of the circumstances surrounding its publication are contained in the introduction. Fragments of the stanza above are repeated throughout the play:
Verse 1 - page 170
Verses 1 & 2 - pages 172, 173, 174 (twice) and 181)

Published: *The Saturday Evening Post* **(July 20, 1911)**
(Volume 184, pages 12-15 and 35-38)

Story: "Devils of Fuatino"
(Part VII, page 123, appears in *A Son of the Sun* **(1912)**)

> Beyond the smiling and the weeping,
>   I shall be soon.
> Beyond the waking and the sleeping,
> Beyond the sowing and the reaping,
>   I shall be soon,
>   I shall be soon.

Attribution: **Horatius Bonar** (1808–1989)
"A Little While"
Verses 1-5 (London repeats verse 5 to make a hexameter.)

Published: *The Cruise of the Snark* **(1911)**
(Before Chapter I)

> You have heard the beat of the offshore wind,
> And the Thresh of the deep-sea rain;
> You have heard the song—how long! how long!
> Pull out on the trail again!

Attribution: **Rudyard Kipling** (1865-1936)
"The Long Tail"
Verses 5-8

Published: *The Cruise of the Snark* (1911)
(Chapter XIV, page 256)

. . . like a summer sky
That held the music of a lark.

Attribution: **George Sterling** (1869-1926)
"The testimony of the Suns" Part II
Verses 322-323

Published: *John Barleycorn* (1913)
(Chapter XVI, page 155)

'Tis but a little golden ring,
I give it to thee with pride,
Wear it for your mother's sake
When you are on the tide.

Attribution: "It is but a little golden Ring."
(The quatrain is adapted from the chorus [8 verses] of a traditional English ballad. Jack London probably saw it on a single broadsheet or a catalogue of broadsheets published by Poet's Box, 224 Overgate, Dundee, Scotland. A catalogue of the same name was printed in 1880.)

Published: *John Barleycorn* (1913)
(Chapter XXXVII, page 330)

Abstain not! Life and Love like night and day,
Offer themselves to us on their own terms,
Not ours. Accept their bounty while ye may,
Before we be accepted by the worms,

Attribution: **William Bliss Carman** (1861-1929) &
Richard Hovey (1864-1900)
Last Songs from Vagabondia, "Quatrains"
Verses 5-8

Published: *John Barleycorn* (1913)
(Chapter XXXVII, page 330)

But if you would not this poor life fulfil,
Lo, you are free to end it when you will,
Without the fear of waking after death.

Attribution: **James Thomson** (1834–82)
"The City of Dreadful Night." Chapter XIV
Verses 82-84

Section C - Poetry in Jack London's Writing Attributed to Others

Published: ***John Barleycorn* (1913)**
(Chapter XXXVII, page 332)

> I heard Youth calling in the night,
> 'Gone is my former world-delight;
> For there is naught my feet may stay;
> The morn suffuses into day,
> It dare not stand a moment still
> But must the world with light fulfil.
> More evanescent than the rose
> My sudden rainbow comes and goes
> Plunging bright ends across the sky—
> Yea, I am Youth because I die!'

Attribution: **Harry Kemp** (1883-1960)
"The Cry of Youth"
Verses 1-10

Published: ***The Valley of the Moon* (1913)**
(After Title page)

> Up, horses, now !
> And straight and true
> Let every broken furrow run :
> The strength you sweat
> Shall blossom yet
> In golden glory to the sun.

Attribution: **Joseph Campbell** (1879-1944)
(alias: **Seosamh MacCathmhaoil** – Irish name)
"Go, Ploughman, Plough"
Verses 8-13

Published: ***The Valley of the Moon* (1913)**
(Book II, Chapter XVIII, page 287)

> O treat my daughter kind-i-ly;
> An' say you'll do no harm,
> An' when I die I'll will to you
> My little house an' farm—
> My horse, my plow, my sheep, my cow,
> An' all them little chickens in the ga-a-rden.

Attribution: **James A. Bland** (1854-1911)
"The Farmer's Daughter" or "The Little Chickens in the Garden" (song title)
This is the Chorus
(Jack London altered the poem as follows:
  i. Verse 1 added "O" to the beginning.
  ii. Verse 2 the word "both" omitted from the end.
  iii. Verse 4 words "stock and" replaced with "house an'."
  iv. Verse 5 the verse reduced from: "My horse, my cow, my sheep, my home, my pump, my barn")

Published: *The Valley of the Moon* **(1913)**
(Book II, Chapter XVIII, page 288)

We'll have a little farm,
A pig, a horse, a cow,
And you will drive the wagon,
And I will drive the plow.

Attribution: **R. Bishop Buckley** (1810-1867)
"Wait for the Wagon" (song)
Verses 3-4 (of 3rd stanza)
(Jack London altered substantially the original song:
   We'll have a little farm, A horse, a pig and cow;
   And you will mind the dairy, While I will guide the plough.)

Published: *Valley of the Moon* **(1913)**
(Book III, Chapter 1, page 305)

Oh! de Judgmen' Day am rollin' roun',
Rollin', yes, a-rollin',
I hear the trumpets' awful soun',
Rollin', yes, a–rollin'.

Attribution: **Elizabeth Banks** (1872–1938)
The Autobiography of a "Newspaper Girl" (1902)
Verses 1-4 – Described in the narrative as, "an old-time darky camp-meeting tune":
(Jack London may have seen it in the book above but may also have seen it in any number of Gospel or Spiritual broad sheets or heard it sung.)

Section C - Poetry in Jack London's Writing Attributed to Others

Published: *The Valley of the Moon* (1913)
(Book III, Chapter I, page 305)

I's gwine back to Dixie,
I's gwine back to Dixie,
I's gwine where de orange blossoms grow,
For I hear de chillun callin',
I see de sad tears fallin'—
My heart's turned back to Dixie,
An' I mus' go.

Attribution: **Charles Albert White** (1830-1892)
"I'se Gwine Back to Dixie" (song) 1878
Entire chorus
(Jack London altered certain words from the original song, maybe to accentuate the ethnicity of the language:
  i. Verse 1, 2 & 3 word "I's" replaces "I'se."
  ii. Verse 3 word "de" replaces "the."
  iii. Verse 4 words "de" replaces "the," "chillun" replaces "children," and "callin'" replaces "calling."
  iv. Verse 5 words "de" replaces "their," and "falling'—" replaces "falling,"
  v. Verse 7 words "An'" replaces "And," and "mus'" replaces "must."

Published: *The Valley of the Moon* (1913)
(Book III, Chapter VI, page 375)

Jesus, Lover of my soul,
Let me to Thy bosom fly,
While the nearer waters roll,
While the tempest still is nigh.
Hide me, O my Saviour, hide,
Till the storm of life is past;
Safe into the haven guide
And receive my soul at last.

Attribution: Words by **Charles Wesley** (1707-1788)
Music by **Joseph Parry** (1841-1903)
"Jesus, Lover of my Soul" (Hymn)
Verses 1-4 (Each verse has been split into two separate verses.)

Published: *The Valley of the Moon* **(1913)**
(Book III, Chapter VIII, page 395)

 Oh! times on Bitter Creek, they never can be beat,
 Root hog or die is on every wagon sheet;
 The sand within your throat, the dust within your eye,
 Bend your back and stand it—root hog or die.

Attribution: **John Hanson Beadle** (1840-1897)
 Life in Utah (Pub. 1870), Chapter VIII—First views in Utah
 "The Bull-Whacker's Epic." Unknown author.
 Verses 210-213

Published: *The Valley of the Moon* **(1913)**
(Book III, Chapter VIII, page 396)

 Obadier, he dreampt a dream,
 Dreampt he was drivin' a ten-mule team,
 But when he woke he heaved a sigh,
 The lead-mule kicked e-o-wt the swing-mule's eye.

Attribution: **John Hanson Beadle** (1840-1897)
 Life in Utah (Published 1870), Chapter VIII—First views in Utah. Unknown Author.
 Verses 176-179

Published: *Valley of the Moon* **(1913)**
(Book III, Chapter VIII, page 397 and 411)

 De Lawd move in er mischievous way
 His blunders to perform.

Attribution: **Will Nathaniel Harben** (1858-1919)
 The Georgians: A Novel (1904)
 Page 40

Published: *The Mutiny of the Elsinore* **(1914)**
(Chapter VIII, pages 49-50)

 Away, way, way, yar,
 We'll kill Paddy Doyle for bus boots.

also

 Then up aloft that yard must go,
 Whiskey for my Johnny.

also

Oh, whiskey killed my sister Sue.

also

And whiskey killed the old man, too,
Whiskey for my Johnny.

Attribution: "Whiskey Johnny," traditional sailing song, "Long Drag Shanty." (Numerous versions exist but this is obviously based upon the traditional shanty.)

Published: ***The Mutiny of the Elsinore*** **(1914)**
(Chapter XIX, pages 133-134)

But they smile innocently and dance on,
Having no thought but this unslumbering thought:
'Am I not beautiful? Shall I not be loved?'
Be patient, for they will not understand,
Not till the end of time will they put by
The weaving of slow steps about men's hearts.

also

They do not understand that in the world
There grows between the sunlight and the grass
Anything save themselves desirable.
It seems to them that the swift eyes of men
Are made but to be mirrors, not to see
Far-off, disastrous, unattainable things.
'For are not we,' they say, 'the end of all?
Why should you look beyond us? If you look
Into the night, you will find nothing there:
We also have gazed often at the stars.

also

We, we alone among all beautiful things,
We only are real: for the rest are dreams.
Why will you follow after wandering dreams
When we await you? And you can but dream
Of us, and in our image fashion them.

Attribution: **Aurthur William Symons** (1865-1945)
Images of Good and Evil: "The Dance of the Daughters of Herodias"

Published: ***The Mutiny of the Elsinore* (1914)**
            (Chapter XXXI, page 200)

    Were I a woman, I would all day long
    Sing my own beauty in some holy song,
    Bend low before it, hushed and half afraid,
    And say 'I am a woman' all day long.

Attribution: **Richard Le Gallienne** (1866-1947)
               Rubáiyát of Omar Khayyám: A Paraphrase from Several Literal Translations, published 1901
               2nd Quatrain on page 46
               (**Le Gallienne** added 50 quatrains to the original 101 written by **Edward FitzGerald** who had discarded many he thought not worthy of inclusion.)

Published: ***The Mutiny of the Elsinore* (1914)**
             (Chapter XXXV, pages 235-236)

    Woman, Man, or God or Devil, was there anything we feared?

    Our bulkheads bulged with cotton and our masts were stepped in gold...
    We ran a mighty merchandise of niggers in the hold...

    By the brand upon my shoulder, by the gall of clinging steel;
    By the welts the whips have left me, by the scars that never heal...
    Battered chain-gangs of the orlop, grizzled draughts of years gone by...

Attribution: **Rudyard Kipling** (1865-1936)
               "The Galley-Slave"
               Verses 20, 5-6, 29-30, & 39
               (These verses are as they appear in the text of Jack London's book.
                  i. Verse 30 originally had a semi-colon at the end.
                  ii. Verse 39 had a comma at the end.)

Published: ***The Star Rover* (1915)**
             (Chapter I, page 2)

    "Not in utter nakedness, not in entire forgetfulness..."

Attribution: **William Wordsworth** (1770-1850)
               "Ode: Intimations of Immortality from Recollections of Early Childhood"
               Verses 63-64
               (This verse is in fact two verses but reversed from original poem)

Section C - Poetry in Jack London's Writing Attributed to Others

Published: *The Star Rover* **(1915)**
(Chapter VI, page 40, also referred to on page 214)

"trailing clouds of glory"

Attribution: **William Wordsworth** (1770-1850)
"Ode: Intimations of Immortality from Recollections of Early Childhood"
Verse 65
(This is an extract from the original verse:
"But trailing clouds of glory do we come.")

Published: *The Star Rover* **(1915)**
(Chapter XI, page 87, 88, 94, and 105)

"Sing cucu, sing cucu, cucu nu nu cucu, sing cucu, sing cucu, sing cucu, sing cucu."

Attribution: **W. de Wycombe** (lived mid 13th Century, probable author)
"Sumer is Icumen," (ca.1260) also known as "The Cuckoo Song."
A medieval English rota song of the mid-13th century.

Published: *The Star Rover* **(1915)**
(Chapter XV, page 179)

No, no, begone! The merry bowl
Again shall bolster up my soul
Against itself. What, good man, hold!
Canst tell me where red wine is sold?
Nay, just beyond yon peach–tree? There?
Good luck be thine; I'll thither fare.

Attribution: Korean Classical "Convivial" Song.
The Korean Repository, (1896) ed. by **F. Ohlinger, George Heber, Jones, H.G. Appenzeller,**, Vol 3, page 49.
Verse 13-18
(Jack London altered the poem:
i. Verse 1 replace "Nay, nay," with "No, no,"
ii. Verse 3 removed dash between "good-man."
iii. Verse 5 inserted dash between "peach tree."
iv. Verse 5 inserted "?" after "peach-tree."
v. Verse 6 replaced comma after "thine" with semi-colon.
Probably translated by **Rev. Homer Bezaleel Hulbert**)

Published: ***The Star Rover* (1915)**
             (Chapter XV, page 203)

    Yanggukeni chajin anga
    Wheanpong tora deunda,
    The thick fog of the Westerners
    Broods over Whean peak.

Attribution: **Homer Bezaleel Hulbert** (1863-1949)
             Passing of Korea (Pub. 1906)
             Verse appears on page 299
             (**Hulbert** collected this Korean song, which refers to a Japanese
             vandal raiding party after gold and treasure in the tombs of
             Tabong Mountain. During the raid there was an unusual thick
             fog over the country which prevented the carrying out of the plan.
             The Korean's composed a popular song about it.)

Published: ***The Little Lady of the Big House* (1916)**
             (Chapter VI, page 71)

    —comrades—
    Old playmates on new seas—
    When as we traded orpiment
    Among the savages—
    A thousand leagues to south'ard
    And thirty years removed—
    They knew not noble Valdez,
    But me they knew and loved.

    Then they that found good liquor
    They drank it not alone,
    And they that found fair plunder,
    They told us every one,
    Behind our chosen islands
    Or secret shoals between,
    When, walty from far voyage,
    We gathered to careen.

    There burned our breaming–fagots,
    All pale along the shore:
    There rose our worn pavilions—
    A sail above an oar:
    As flashed each yearning anchor
    Through mellow seas afire,

So swift our careless captains
Rowed each to his desire.

Where lay our loosened harness?
Where turned our naked feet?
Whose tavern mid the palm-trees?
What quenchings of what heat?
Oh fountain in the desert!
Oh cistern in the waste!
Oh bread we ate in secret!
Oh cup we spilled in haste!

The youth new-taught of longing,
The widow curbed and wan—
The good wife proud at season,
And the maid aware of man;
All souls, unslaked, consuming,
Defrauded in delays,
Desire not more than quittance
Than I those forfeit days!'

I dreamed to wait my pleasure,
Unchanged my spring would bide:
Wherefore, to wait my pleasure,
I put my spring aside,
Till, first in face of Fortune,
And last in mazed disdain,
I made Diego Valdez
High Admiral of Spain!

Attribution: **Rudyard Kipling** (1865-1936)
The Five Nations: "The Song Diego Valdez"
Verses 17-64

Published: ***The Little Lady of the Big House* (1916)**
(Chapter VI, pages 72-73)

There walks no wind 'neath heaven
Nor wave that shall restore
The old careening riot
And the clamorous, crowded shore—
The fountain in the desert,
The cistern in the waste,

The bread we ate in secret,
The cup we spilled in haste.

Attribution: **Rudyard Kipling** (1865-1936)
*The Five Nation*s: "The Song Diego Valdez"
Verses 81-88

Published: *The Little Lady of the Big House* **(1916)**
(Chapter VI, pages 77-78)

Hu'-tim yo'-kim koi-o-di'!
Wi'-hi yan'-ning koi-o-di'!
Lo'-whi yan'-ning koi-o-di'!
Yo-ho' Nai-ni', hal-u'-dom yo nai, yo-ho' nai-nim'!

The acorns come down from heaven!
I plant the short acorns in the valley!
I plant the long acorns in the valley!
I sprout, I, the black-oak acorn, sprout, I sprout!"

Attribution: **Stephen Powers** (1840-1904)
Tribes of California (Pub. 1877)
(**Powers** reported this song or chant of the Indian tribes of the San Franciscan Bay Area. This work was later turned into the Ethnological Report, Vol. 3, the US Pacific Coast Geographical and Geological Survey referred to by Jack London in the text.)

Published: *Little Lady of the Big House* **(1916)**
(Chapter VIII, page 91)

The goldfish thwimmeth in the bowl,
The robin thiths upon the tree;
What maketh them thit so eathily?
Who stuckth the fur upon their breasths?
God! God! He done it!

Attribution: (This hexameter poem is an adaptation (possibly London's own) from a poem contained within a humorous piece by an unattributed author on page 163 of *Among the Humorists and After- dinner Speakers: A New Collection of Humorous Stories and Anecdotes* (Pub. 1909, Vol. 1), edited by **William Patten** (1868-1936). It is possible that London heard it from some other source but this proves beyond doubt that it was known and published before Jack London's book. Jack London altered the original extensively and is reprinted here to compare:

Section C - Poetry in Jack London's Writing Attributed to Others

> "See the pretty gold fish swimming in the Globe!
> See the pretty robin singing in the tree!
> Who teached these two to fly together?
> Who stucked the fur upon their breasts?
> 'Twas God. 'Twas God. He done it."

Published: ***The Little Lady of the Big House* (1916)**
       (Chapter XVII, pages 213-215)

Follow the Romany patteran
  West to the sinking sun,
Till the junk sails lift through the homeless drift,
  And the East and the West are one. (*Stanza 9*)

also

Back to the road again, again,
  Out of a clear sea track;
Follow the cross of the Gypsy trail,
  Over the world and back. (*Stanza 6*)

also

The wild hawk to the wind-swept sky,
  The deer to the wholesome wold,
And the heart of a man to the heart of a maid
  As it was in the days of old— (*Stanza 11*)

The heart of a man to the heart of a maid,
  Light of my tents be fleet,
Morning waits at the end of the world,
  And the world is all at our feet. (*Stanza 12*)

Attribution: **Rudyard Kipling** (1865-1936)
       The Years Between: "Gypsy Trail"
       Verses: 33-36, 24-27, & 41-48 (45-48 also repeated in chapter
       XXXI, page 389 with a slightly different verse structure)
       (Jack London altered the following:
         i. Verse 24 first word "Both" changed to "Back."
         ii. Verse 44 a dash replaces a comma.
         iii. Verse 48 a full stop replaces an explanation mark.)

Published: ***The Little Lady of the Big House* (1916)**
       (Chapter XXXI, page 380)

> Fer itself, fer itself,
> Fer itself, fer itself,
> Every soul got ter confess
> Fer itself.

Attribution: This extract is the first stanza of a negro spiritual (author unknown), which appears in an article by **Lucine Finch** called "A Sermon in Parchwork," published in the *Outlook Magazine*, October 28, 1914.

Published: *Michael, Brother of Jerry* **(1917)**
(Chapter XXXII, page 292)

> A Robin Redbreast in a cage
> Puts all heaven in a rage.

Attribution: **William Blake** (1757-1827)
"Auguies of Innocence"
Verses 6-7

Published: *Cosmopolitan* **(September 1918)**
(Volume 65, pages 32-37 and 135-138)

Story: "The Water Baby"
(Page 153, appears in *On the Makaloa Mat* **(1919)**)

> Give to me the trunk of the tree, O Lono!
> Give me the tree's main root, O Lono!
> Give me the ear of the tree, O Lono!—

Attribution: Mythological Song of the Hawaiian God Lono.
First published by **Hiram Bingham** (1789–1869) in his book *A Residence of Twenty-One Years in the Sandwich Islands* (1848) Pages 222, Verses 1-3.
(Three stanzas were printed of probably 30. The rest being considered "...adapted to a gross heathen state, and is unfit to appear in English dress." Bingham, being a methodist missionary, felt unable to print the full song because it was so unacceptable to his religious sensibilities. Jack London may have seen this reprinted in the numerous magazines related to stories of Hawaii. Jack London altered the poem:
i. Verse 1 replaced emdash at the end with explanation mark.
ii. Verse 2 replaced emdash at the end with explanation mark.
iii. Verse 3 replaced full stop with explanation mark and emdash.)

Published: ***Hearts of Three* (London, 1918)**
(After the Preface)
(This poem was omitted from the USA edition published in 1920)

Back to Back Against the Mainmast

Do ye seek for fun and fortune?
Listen, rovers, now to me !
Look ye for them on the ocean :
Ye shall find them on the sea.

CHORUS :
   Roaring wind and deep blue water!
   We're the jolly devils who,
   Back to back against the mainmast,
   Held at bay the entire crew.

Bring the dagger, bring the pistols!
We will have our own to–day!
Let the cannon smash the bulwarks!
Let the cutlass clear the way!

CHORUS : (as above)

Here's to rum and here's to plunder!
Here's to all the gales that blow!
Let the seamen cry for mercy!
Let the blood of captain's flow!

CHORUS : (as above)
Here's to ships that we have taken!
They have seen which men were best.
We have lifted maids and cargo,
And the sharks have had the rest.

CHORUS : (as above)

Attribution: **George Sterling** (1869-1926)
"Back to Back Against the Mainmast"
Verses: entire poem
(Referred to in a **George Sterling** letter to Jack London, Oct 1916, as the "Pirate Song." In the UK and USA editions verses 3 and 4 of the chorus are repeated in:
   Chapter II, page 21

Chapter II, page 22 (twice)
Chapter II, page 23
Chapter III, page 41
Chapter XVII, page 175 (twice)
Chapter XXIII, page 231
Chapter XXIX, page 290)

Published: *Hearts of Three* **(London, 1918)**
(Chapter XIX, page 190)

No wedding bells for me,
I'm as happy as can be . . .

Attribution: Words by: **E. P Moran & Will A. Heelan** (birth dates unknown).
Music by: **Seymour Furth** (1877-1932)
Song: "No Wedding Bells for me," copyright 1906, by **Maurice Shapiro**, Broadway & 89th St., New York.
Verses: Opening verses of the Chorus

Published: *Cosmopolitan* **(September 1918)**
(Volume 65, pages 80-85 and 133)

Story: "The Water Baby"
(Page 143, appears in *On the Makaloa Mat* **(1919)**)

Maui became restless and fought the sun
With a noose that he laid.
And winter won the sun,
And summer was won by Maui.

Attribution: **William Drake Westervelt** (1849-1939)
Legends of Ma-Ui—A Demi God of Polynesia and of his Mother Hina (1910), Chapter IV, page 40. (Queen Liliuokalani's family chant)
Entire verse.

Published: *Cosmopolitan* **(September 1918)**
(Volume 65, pages 80-85 and 133)

Story: "The Water Baby"
(Pages 145-146, appears in *On the Makaloa Mat* **(1919)**)

Oh, the great fishhook of Maui!
Manai–i–ka–lani—"made fast to the heavens"!
An earth–twisted cord ties the hook,

Section C - Poetry in Jack London's Writing Attributed to Others

Engulfed from lofty Kauiki!
Its bait the red–billed Alae,
The bird to Hina sacred!
It sinks far down to Hawaii,
Struggling and in pain dying!
Caught is the land beneath the water,
Floated up, up to the surface,
But Hina hid a wing of the bird
And broke the land beneath the water!
Below was the bait snatched away
And eaten at once by the fishes,
The Ulua of the deep muddy places!

Attribution:	**William Drake Westervelt** (1849-1939) *Legends of Ma–Ui—A Demi God of Polynesia and of his Mother Hina* (1910), Chapter II, page 12. (Chant of Kualii) Entire poem.
Published:	*Cosmopolitan* **(September 1918)** (Volume 65, pages 80-85 and 133)
Story:	"The Water Baby" (Pages 148-149, appears in *On the Makaloa Mat* **(1919)**)

O Kanaloa of the taboo nights!
Stand upright on the solid floor!
Stand upon the floor where lies the squid!
Stand up to take the squid of the deep sea!
Rise up, O Kanaloa!
Stir up! Stir up! Let the squid awake!
Let the squid that lies flat awake!
Let the squid that lies spread out. . . .

Attribution:	**June Gutmanis (1926-1998)** *Na Pule Kahiko: Ancient Hawaiian Prayers*, (Pub. 1983), An ancient Hawaian fishman's morning prayer. Page 6, verses 5-12. (Jack London may have heard it while in Hawaii.)
Published:	*Cosmopolitan* **(November 1918)** (Volume 65, pages 74-81 & 119-121)
Story:	"In the Cave of the Dead" (Page 106, subsequently appears as "Shin Bones" in *On the Makaloa Mat* **(1919)**)

> They have gone down to the pit with their weapons of war, and they have laid their swords under their heads.

Attribution: This appears to be a truncated version of *Ezekiel 32-27* (King James Bible). The full version is as follows:

> 27. And they shall not lie with the mighty that are fallen of the uncircumcised, which are gone down to hell with their weapons of war: and they have laid their swords under their heads, but their iniquities shall be upon their bones, though they were the terror of the mighty in the land of the living.

Published: ***Cosmopolitan* (July 1919)**
(Volume 67, pages 95-100, 102 and 104)

Story: "The Bones of Kahekili"
(Page 72, appears in *On the Makaloa Mat* **(1919)**)

> But death is nothing new.
> Death is and has been ever since old Maui died.
> Then Pata-tai laughed loud
> And woke the goblin-god,
> Who severed him in two, and shut him in,
> So dusk of eve came on.

Attribution: **William Drake Westervelt** (1849-1939)
Legends of Ma-Ui – A Demi God of Polynesia and of his Mother Hina (1910): Chapter XI: "Maui Seeking Immortality" page 138. (Maori death chant)
Entire poem.

SECTION D

VERSE IN JACK LONDON'S WRITING UNATTRIBUTED TO OTHERS

In this section we have gathered all the verse that appears in Jack London's writing, whether fiction or nonfiction, which is unattributed to any other author or previously published and which could possibly be written by Jack London. This also includes a number of complete poems, pieces of verse, or adaptations from verse that were written by Jack London and previously published.

1. **Published**: This refers to the first publication in which the verse appears and will be in bold and italicized, omitted when not published. In the case of individual stories, this covers a wide range of publications from magazines to newspapers, periodicals and first edition books. All citings are with volume, chapter and page as appropriate.

2. **Story**: Where applicable this refers to the particular Jack London book, story, essay or play in which the verse appears. The story, essay or play will be in quotes plus chapter and page from the first edition book as appropriate in parenthesis.

3. Verses or Song Lyrics as they appear when first published.

4. **Attribution**: Where possible the following information is provided:

    a. Author of the verse.
    b. Book (in italics) and poem (in quotes).
    c. Verses from full poem.
    d. Any other notes or comments (in parenthesis).

Story: "Strange Experiences of a Misogynist"
(Written in 1897 appears on page 66 of *The Complete Short Stories of Jack London* (1993))

> Here's to the good old whiskey, drink it down!
> Here's to the good old whiskey, drink it down!
> Here's to the good old whiskey,
> For it makes you feel so frisky,
> Drink it down! Drink it down! Drink it down!

Attribution: Author unknown therefore possibly written by Jack London. "Drink it Down" is a traditional American drinking song found in many variants, including fraternity and military song books. **Charles Samuel Elliot**'s 1870, *Songs of Yale: A New Collection of College Songs,* "Bingo" page 40, contains one of the earliest versions. So popular was the song that The Salvation Army set the music to the words "Storm the Forts of Darkness, Bring Them Down," by **Robert Johnson**, which is still played today.

Published: *Overland Monthly* **(January 1899)**
(Volume 33, pages 36-40)

Story: "To the Man on Trail"
(Pages 104-105, appears in *The Son of the Wolf* (1900))

> There's Henry Ward Beecher
> And Sunday-school teachers,
> All drink of the sassafras root;
> But you bet all the same,
> If it had its right name,
> It's the juice of the forbidden fruit.
>
> Oh the juice of the forbidden fruit;
> But you bet all the same,
> If it had its right name,
> It's the juice of the forbidden fruit.

Attribution: Author unknown therefore possibly written by Jack London. A slight variation of this poem also appears in *Burning Daylight* **(1910)**, Part I, Chapter III, page 35.

Published: *Town Topics* (New York) (Apr 26, 1899)
(Volume XLIII, 19, page 23)

Book: *Martin Eden* **(1909)**
(Chapter XXII, page 189)

Section D - Poetry in Jack London's Writing Unattributed to Others

> He came in
> When I was out,
> To borrow some tin
> Was why he came in,
> And he went without;
> So I was in
> And he was out.

Attribution: This is Jack London's triolet poem "When He Came In" (page 9). The first word "When" and verse 5 are omitted from the original. London completed this poem on January 23, 1899. It was also reprinted in *Town Topics* on May 10, 1910 as "In and Out."

Published: *The Atlantic Monthly* **(January 1900)**
(Volume 85, pages 85-100)

Story: "An Odyssey of the North"
(Page 211, appears in *The Son of the Wolf* (1900))

> Yank–kee ship come down de ri–ib–er,
> Pull! my bully boys! Pull!
> D'yeh want — to know de captain ru–uns her?
> Pull! my bully boys! Pull!
> Jon–a–than Jones ob South Caho–li–in–a,
> Pull! my bully"

Attribution: The structure of this extract is based on a tradition Sea Shanty called "Blow Boys, Blow!" Used as work songs for sailing ships called "halyard chanteys," also "single pull" or "long haul" chanteys. Jack London may have written this version.

Published: *Outing* **(Albany, N.Y.) (December 1900)**
(Volume 37, page 276-282)

Story: "Where the Trail Forks"
(Page 188, appears in *The God of His Fathers* (1901))

> In a year, in a year, when the grapes are ripe,
> I shall stay no more away.
> Then if you still are true, my love,
> It will be our wedding day.
> In a year, in a year, when my time is past,
> Then I'll live in your love for aye.
> Then if you still are true, my love,
> It will be our wedding day.

Attribution: Jack London wrote this and it appears in Section A: Jack

London's Published Poetry, page 17, of this book as "In a Year."
Verses 1-2 also appear on page 194, Verse 1 again on page 208.

Published: ***The Pittsburg (Pa.) Labor Leader***, **(March 24, 1901)**
(Page.31)

Story: "At the Rainbow's End"
(Page 247, appears in ***The God of His Fathers*** (1901))

> Wonder if it's true ?
> Does it seem so to you ?
> Seems to me he's lying—
> Oh, I wonder if it's true? (*This verse repeated on the same page*)

Attribution: Author unknown therefore possibly written by Jack London.

Published: ***Hampton's Magazine*** **(New York) (March 1911)**
(Volume 26, pages 309-318)

Story: "The Strength of the Strong"
(Page 1, appears in ***The Strength of the Strong*** (1914))

> **Parables don't lie, but liars will parable—Lip–King**

Attribution: Author unknown therefore possibly written by Jack London. The last word is an anagram of **Kipling**, who was one of London's favorite poets.

Published: ***Cosmopolitan*** **(July 1911)**
(Volume 51, pages 209-222)

Story: "The Meat"
(Page 64, appears in ***Smoke Bellew*** (1912))

> Like Argus of the ancient times,
> We leave this Modern Greece,
> Tum-tum, tum-tum; tum-tum, tum-tum,
> To shear the Golden Fleece.

Attribution: Unknown author therefore possibly written by Jack London. Also appears in the story "Like Argus of the Ancient Times," and the book ***The Red One***.

Published: ***John Barleycorn*** **(1913)**
(Chapter VII, page 68)

> Oh, it's Lulu, black Lulu, my darling,
> Oh, it's where have you been so long?

Section D - Poetry in Jack London's Writing Unattributed to Others

> Been layin' in jail,
> A–waitin' for bail,
> Till my bully comes rollin' along.

Attribution: Unknown author therefore possibly written by Jack London.

Published: *Valley of the Moon* (1913)
(Book I, Chapter VI, pages 48-49)

> Sweet as a wind–lute's airy strains
> Your gentle muse has learned to sing,
> And California's boundless plains
> Prolong the soft notes echoing.

(This stanza is also repeated in Book II, chapter XIV, page 297 and Book III, Chapter III, page 344.)

also

> I have stolen away from the crowd in the groves,
> Where the nude statues stand, and the leaves point and shiver
> At ivy–crowned Bacchus, the Queen of the Loves,
> Pandora and Psyche, struck voiceless forever.

(The first and second verse of this stanza also appear on page 344.)

also

> The dusk of the greenhouse is luminous yet
> With quivers of opal and tremors of gold;
> For the sun is at rest, and the light from the west,
> Like delicate wine that is mellow and old,
>
> Flushes faintly the brow of a naiad that stands
> In the spray of a fountain, whose seed-amethysts
> Tremble lightly a moment on bosom and hands,
> Then drip in their basin from bosom and wrists.

(The second, third and fourth verse of this stanza also appear on page 344.)

Attribution: Unknown author therefore possibly written by Jack London.

Published: *Valley of the Moon* (1913)
(Book I, Chapter XIV, page 114)

> And when I work, and when I work,
> I'll always work for Billy.

Attribution: Unknown author therefore possibly written by Jack London.

Published: *Valley of the Moon* (1913)
(Book II, Chapter VII, page 169)

> Nobody loves a mil-yun-aire.
> Nobody likes his looks.
> Nobody'll share his slightest care,
> He classes with thugs and crooks.
> Thriftiness has become a crime,
> So spend everything you earn;
> We're living now in a funny time,
> When money is made to burn.

Attribution: Unknown author therefore possibly written by Jack London. Verses 1-4 repeated on pages 172 & 173, verses 7-8 repeated on page 171.

Published: *The Star Rover* (1915)
(Chapter XIII, page 140)

> Said the first little devil to the second little devil,
> 'Give me some tobaccy from your old tobaccy box.'
> Said the second little devil to the first little devil,
> 'Stick close to your money and close to your rocks,
> An' you'll always have tobaccy in your old tobaccy box.'

Attribution: There are many versions of this song with the ending verse "...tobaccy in your old tobaccy box." The original author is unknown but is probably a mining or prospecting song. Jack London may have written this particular version.

Published: *Cosmopolitan* (September 1915)
(Volume 59, No 4, pages 520-536)

Story: Appeared in *Little Lady of the Big House* (1916)
(Chapter XX, page 247)

> What can little Paula do?
> Why, drive a phaeton and two.
> Can little Paula do no more?
> Yes, drive a tally-ho and four.

Attribution: Author unknown therefore possibly written by Jack London.

Published: *Little Lady of the Big House* (1916)
(Chapter X, pages 120-121)

> Me, I am Ai-kut,
> the first man of the Nishinam.

Ai-kut is the short for Adam,
and my father and my mother
were the coyote and the moon.
And this is Yo-to-to-wi, my wife.
She is the first woman of the Nishinam.
(*Verses 1-7 repeated in Chapter XXXI, page 389-390*)

Her father and her mother were the
grasshopper and the ring-tailed cat.
They were the best father and mother
left after my father and mother.
The coyote is very wise,
the moon is very old;
but who ever heard much of
anything of credit to the
grasshopper and the ring-tailed cat?
The Nishinam are always right.
The mother of all women had to be a cat,
a little, wizened, sad-faced,
shrewd ring-tailed cat.

also

This is Yo-to-to-wi,
which is the short for Eve,
Yo-to-to-wi is not much to look at.
But be not hard upon her.
The fault is with the grasshopper
and the ring-tailed cat.
Me, I am Ai-kut, the first man;
but question not my taste.
I was the first man, and this,
I saw, was the first woman.
Where there is but one choice,
there is not much to choose.
Adam was so circumstanced.
He chose Eve.
Yo-to-to-wi was the one woman
in all the world for me,
so I chose Yo-to-to-wi.

Me, I am Ai-kut,
This is my dew of woman.
She is my honey-dew of woman.
I have lied to you.
Her father and her mother
were neither hopper nor cat.

They were the Sierra dawn and
the summer east wind of the mountains.
Together they conspired,
and from the air and earth
they sweated all sweetness
till in a mist of their own love
the leaves of the chaparral
and the manzanita were dewed
with the honey-dew.
(*Stanza repeated with slight variation in Chapter XXXI, page 390*)

Yo-to-to-wi is my honey-dew woman.
Hear me ! I am Ai-kut !
Yo-to-to-wi is my quail woman,
my deer-woman,
my lush-woman of all soft rain and fat soil.
She was born of the thin starlight
and the brittle dawn-light before the sun . . .
(*Stanza repeated in Chapter XXXI, page 390, but with altered ending:*

and the brittle dawn-light in the morning
of the world, and she is the one woman
of all women to me.)

Attribution: The preceding song, which appears in text narrative form in *The Little Lady of the Big House*, has been restated in a verse structure parallel to that of "The Song of the First Man" as it appears in *The Acorn Planter* (pages 10-13). It is, in fact, a thinly disguised restatement of that song with the first two verses being identical except for the character of Red Cloud being changed to that of Ai-kut. This restatement clearly demonstrates the parallelism. London wrote these two books concurrently (*The Acorn Planter* was published in February 1916 and *The Little Lady of the Big House* was published in April 1916) such that this "duplication" is no surprise.

Published: *Little Lady of the Big House* **(1916)**
(Chapter XVI, page 193 & 194)

Jong-Keena, Jong-Keena,
Jong-Jong, Keena-Keena,
Yo-ko-ham-a, Nag-a-sak-i,
Kobe-mar-o — hoy! ! !

Attribution: Author unknown therefore possibly written by Jack London. However, the narrative suggests a Japanese tradition song.

SECTION E

PLAY

THE ACORN PLANTER

This section and the next contain two plays written in verse and published by Jack London: *The Acorn Planter* and *The First Poet*. They are included in this book not solely because they are verse, but because they confirm London's life long attraction to poetic verse as a vehicle for expression.

The Acorn Planter was definitely written by Jack London. This play was published in February 1916. It was written for the "High Jinks" festivities at the Bohemian Club, but it was not performed until August 1, 2001 at Sonoma State University.

As noted in the "Attributed Poetry" section, London was an admirer of Longfellow and frequently quoted him in his own writings. It is, therefore, probably not a coincidence that this play is written, in parts, in the style of Longfellow's "The Song of Hiawatha" in trochaic tetrameter and likely inspired by that poem.

On the title page of the first edition of *The Acorn Planter*, London instructs that the play is "to be sung by efficient singers accompanied by a capable orchestra." Given that this is a "play in verse," this statement again demonstrates the fungibility of song and poetry in London's mind.

THE ACORN PLANTER
A CALIFORNIA FOREST PLAY

ARGUMENT

In the morning of the world, while his tribe makes its camp for the night in a grove, Red Cloud, the first man of men, and the first man of the Nishinam, save in war, sings of the duty of life, which duty is to make life more abundant. The Shaman, or medicine man, sings of foreboding and prophecy. The War Chief, who commands in war, sings that war is the only way to life. This Red Cloud denies, affirming that the way of life is the way of the acorn-planter, and that whoso slays one man slays the planter of many acorns. Red Cloud wins the Shaman and the people to his contention.

After the passage of thousands of years, again in the grove appear the Nishinam. In Red Cloud, the War Chief, the Shaman, and the Dew-Woman are repeated the eternal figures of the philosopher, the soldier, the priest, and the woman—types ever realizing themselves afresh in the social adventures of man. Red Cloud recognizes the wrecked explorers as planters and life-makers, and is for treating them with kindness. But the War Chief and the idea of war are dominant. The Shaman joins with the war party, and is privy to the massacre of the explorers.

A hundred years pass, when, on their seasonal migration, the Nishinam camp for the night in the grove. They still live, and the war formula for life seems vindicated, despite the imminence of the superior life-makers, the whites, who are flooding into California from north, south, east, and west—the English, the Americans, the Spaniards, and the Russians. The massacre by the white men follows, and Red Cloud, dying, recognizes the white men as brother acorn-planters, the possessors of the superior life-formula of which he had always been a protagonist.

In the Epilogue, or Apotheosis, occur the celebration of the death of war and the triumph of the acorn-planters.

PROLOGUE

TIME. *In the morning of the world.*

SCENE. *A forest hillside where great trees stand with wide spaces between. A stream flows from a spring that bursts out of the hillside. It is a place of lush ferns and brakes, also, of thickets of such shrubs as inhabit a redwood forest floor. At the left, in the open level space at the foot of the hillside, extending out of sight among the trees, is visible a portion of a Nishinam Indian camp. It is a temporary camp for the night. Small cooking fires smoulder. Standing about are withe-woven baskets for the carrying of supplies and dunnage. Spears and bows and quivers of arrows lie about. Boys drag in dry branches for firewood. Young women fill gourds with water from the stream and proceed about their camp tasks. A number of older women are pounding acorns in stone mortars with stone pestles. An old man and a Shaman, or priest, look expectantly up the hillside. All wear moccasins and are skin-clad, primitive, in their garmenting. Neither iron nor woven cloth occurs in the weapons and gear.*

SHAMAN

(*Looking up hillside.*)
Red Cloud is late.

OLD MAN

(*After inspection of hillside.*)
He has chased the deer far. He is patient. In the chase he is patient like an old man.

SHAMAN

His feet are as fleet as the deer's.

OLD MAN

(*Nodding.*)
And he is more patient than the deer.

SHAMAN

(Assertively, as if inculcating a lesson.)
He is a mighty chief.

OLD MAN

(Nodding.)
His father was a mighty chief. He is like to his father.

SHAMAN

(More assertively.)
He is his father. It is so spoken. He is his father's father. He is the first man, the first Red Cloud, ever born, and born again, to chiefship of his people.

OLD MAN

It is so spoken.

SHAMAN

His father was the Coyote. His mother was the Moon. And he was the first man.

OLD MAN

(Repeating.)
His father was the Coyote. His mother was the Moon. And he was the first man.

SHAMAN

He planted the first acorns, and he is very wise.

OLD MAN

(Repeating.)
He planted the first acorns, and he is very wise.

(Cries from the women and a turning of faces. RED

CLOUD *appears among his hunters descending the hillside. All carry spears, and bows and arrows. Some carry rabbits and other small game. Several carry deer.*)

PLAINT OF THE NISHINAM

Red Cloud, the meat-bringer !
Red Cloud, the acorn-planter !
Red Cloud, first man of the Nishinam !
Thy people hunger.
Far have they fared.
Hard has the way been.
Day long they sought,
High in the mountains,
Deep in the pools,
Wide 'mong the grasses,
In the bushes, and tree-tops,
Under the earth and flat stones.
Few are the acorns,
Past is the time for berries,
Fled are the fishes, the prawns and the grass-hoppers,
Blown far are the grass-seeds,
Flown far are the young birds,
Old are the roots and withered.
Built are the fires for the meat.
Laid are the boughs for sleep,
Yet thy people cannot sleep.
Red Cloud, thy people hunger.

RED CLOUD

(*Still descending.*)
Good hunting !   Good hunting !

HUNTERS

Good hunting !   Good hunting !

(*Completing the descent,* RED CLOUD *motions to the meat-bearers. They throw down their burdens before the women, who greedily inspect the spoils.*)

MEAT SONG OF THE NISHINAM

Meat that is good to eat,
Tender for old teeth,
Gristle for young teeth,
Big deer and fat deer,
Lean meat and fat meat,
Haunch-meat and knuckle-bone,
Liver and heart.
Food for the old men,
Life for all men,
For women and babes.
Easement of hunger-pangs,
Sorrow destroying,
Laughter provoking,
Joy invoking,
In the smell of its smoking
And its sweet in the mouth.

(*The younger women take charge of the meat, and the older women resume their acorn-pounding.*)

(RED CLOUD *approaches the acorn-pounders and watches them with pleasure. All group about him, the* SHAMAN *to the fore, and hang upon his every action, his every utterance.*)

RED CLOUD

The heart of the acorn is good?

FIRST OLD WOMAN

(*Nodding.*)
It is good food.

RED CLOUD

When you have pounded and winnowed and washed away the bitter.

SECOND OLD WOMAN

As thou taught'st us, Red Cloud, when the world was very young and thou wast the first man.

RED CLOUD

It is a fat food. It makes life, and life is good.

SHAMAN

It was thou, Red Cloud, gathering the acorns and teaching the storing, who gavest life to the Nishinam in the lean years aforetime, when the tribes not of the Nishinam passed like the dew of the morning.
 (*He nods a signal to the* OLD MAN.)

OLD MAN

In the famine in the old time,
When the old man was a young man,
When the heavens ceased from raining,
When the grasslands parched and withered,
When the fishes left the river,
And the wild meat died of sickness,
In the tribes that knew not acorns,
All their women went dry-breasted,
All their younglings chewed the deer-hides,
All their old men sighed and perished,
And the young men died beside them,
Till they died by tribe and totem,
And o'er all was death upon them.
Yet the Nishinam unvanquished,
Did not perish by the famine.
Oh, the acorns Red Cloud gave them !
Oh, the acorns Red Cloud taught them
How to store in willow baskets
'Gainst the time and need of famine !

SHAMAN

(*Who, throughout the* OLD MAN'S *recital, has nodded approbation, turning to* RED CLOUD.)
Sing to thy people, Red Cloud, the song of life which is the song of the acorn.

RED CLOUD

(*Making ready to begin.*)
And which is the song of woman, O Shaman.

SHAMAN

(*Hushing the people to listen, solemnly.*)
He sings with his father's lips, and with the lips of his father's fathers to the beginning of time and men.

SONG OF THE FIRST MAN

RED CLOUD

I am Red Cloud,
The first man of the Nishinam.
My father was the Coyote.
My mother was the Moon.
The Coyote danced with the stars,
And wedded the Moon on a mid-summer night.

The Coyote is very wise,
The Moon is very old,
Mine is his wisdom,
Mine is her age.
I am the first man.
I am the life-maker and the father of life.

I am the fire-bringer.
The Nishinam were the first men,
And they were without fire,
And knew the bite of the frost of bitter nights.
The panther stole the fire from the East,
The fox stole the fire from the panther,

The ground squirrel stole the fire from the fox,
And I, Red Cloud, stole the fire from the ground squirrel.
I, Red Cloud, stole the fire for the Nishinam,
And hid it in the heart of the wood.
To this day is the fire there in the heart of the wood.

I am the Acorn-Planter.
I brought down the acorns from heaven.
I planted the short acorns in the valley.
I planted the long acorns in the valley.
I planted the black-oak acorns that sprout, that sprout !

I planted the *sho-kum* and all the roots of the ground.
I planted the oat and the barley, the beaver-tail grass-nut,
The tar-weed and crow-foot, rock lettuce and ground lettuce,
And I taught the virtue of clover in the season of blossom,
The yellow-flowered clover, ball-rolled in its yellow dust.
I taught the cooking in baskets by hot stones from the fire,
Took the bite from the buckeye and soap-root
By ground-roasting and washing in the sweetness of water,
And of the manzanita the berry I made into flour,
Taught the way of its cooking with hot stones in sand pools,
And the way of its eating with the knobbed tail of the deer.

Taught I likewise the gathering and storing,
The parching and pounding
Of the seeds from the grasses and grass-roots ;
And taught I the planting of seeds in the Nishinam home-camps,
In the Nishinam hills and their valleys,
In the due times and seasons,
To sprout in the spring rains and grow ripe in the sun.

SHAMAN

Hail, Red Cloud, the first man !

THE PEOPLE

Hail, Red Cloud, the first man !

Shaman

Who showedst us the way of our feet in the world!

The People

Who showedst us the way of our feet in the world!

Shaman
Who showedst us the way of our food in the world!

The People

Who showedst us the way of our food in the world!

Shaman

Who showedst us the way of our hearts in the world!

The People

Who showedst us the way of our hearts in the world!

Shaman

Who gavest us the law of family!

The People

Who gavest us the law of family!

Shaman

The law of tribe!

The People

The law of tribe!

Shaman

The law of totem!

THE PEOPLE

The law of totem !

SHAMAN

And madest us strong in the world among men !

THE PEOPLE

And madest us strong in the world among men !

RED CLOUD

Life is good, O Shaman, and I have sung but half its song. Acorns are good. So is woman good. Strength is good. Beauty is good. So is kindness good. Yet are all these things without power except for woman. And by these things woman makes strong men, and strong men make for life, ever for more life.

WAR CHIEF

(With gesture of interruption that causes remonstrance from the SHAMAN but which RED CLOUD acknowledges.)
I care not for beauty. I desire strength in battle and wind in the chase that I may kill my enemy and run down my meat.

RED CLOUD

Well spoken, O War Chief. By voices in council we learn our minds, and that, too, is strength. Also, is it kindness. For kindness and strength and beauty are one. The eagle in the high blue of the sky is beautiful. The salmon leaping the white water in the sunlight is beautiful. The young man fastest of foot in the race is beautiful. And because they fly well, and leap well, and run well, are they beautiful. Beauty must beget beauty. The ring-tail cat begets the ring-tail cat, the dove the dove. Never does the dove beget the ring-tail cat. Hearts must be kind. The little turtle is not kind. That is why it is the little turtle. It lays its eggs in the sun-warm sand and forgets its young forever. And the little turtle is forever the little turtle. But we are not little turtles, because we are kind. We do not leave our young to the sun in the sand. Our women keep our young warm under their hearts, and, after, they keep them warm with deer-skin and campfire. Because we are kind we are men and not little turtles, and that is why we eat the little turtle that is not strong because it is not kind.

WAR CHIEF

(*Gesturing to be heard.*)
The Modoc come against us in their strength. Often the Modoc come against us. We cannot be kind to the Modoc.

RED CLOUD

That will come after. Kindness grows. First must we be kind to our own. After, long after, all men will be kind to all men, and all men will be very strong. The strength of the Nishinam is not the strength of its strongest fighter. It is the strength of all the Nishinam added together that makes the Nishinam strong. We talk, you and I, War Chief and First Man, because we are kind one to the other, and thus we add together our wisdom, and all the Nishinam are stronger because we have talked.
(*A voice is heard singing.* RED CLOUD *holds up his hand for silence.*)

MATING SONG

DEW-WOMAN

In the morning by the river,
  In the evening at the fire,
In the night when all lay sleeping,
  Torn was I with life's desire.
There were stirrings 'neath my heart-beats
  Of the dreams that came to me ;
In my ears were whispers, voices,
  Of the children yet to be.

RED CLOUD

(As RED CLOUD *sings,* DEW-WOMAN *steals from behind a tree and approaches him.)*

In the morning by the river
  Saw I first my maid of dew,
Daughter of the dew and dawnlight,
  Of the dawn and honey-dew.
She was laughter, she was sunlight,
  Woman, maid, and mate, and wife ;
She was sparkle, she was gladness,
  She was all the song of life.

DEW-WOMAN

In the night I built my fire,
  Fire that maidens foster when
In the ripe of mating season
  Each builds for her man of men.

RED CLOUD

In the night I sought her, proved her,
  Found her ease, content, and rest,
After day of toil and struggle
  Man's reward on woman's breast.

DEW-WOMAN

Came to me my mate and lover ;
  Kind the hands he laid on me ;
Wooed me gently as a man may,
  Father of the race to be.

RED CLOUD

Soft her arms about me bound me,
  First man of the Nishinam,
Arms as soft as dew and dawnlight,
  Daughter of the Nishinam.

RED CLOUD

She was life and she was woman!

DEW-WOMAN

He was life and he was man!

RED CLOUD AND DEW-WOMAN

(*Arms about each other.*)
In the dusk-time of our love-night,
   There beside the marriage fire,
Proved we all the sweets of living,
   In the arms of our desire.

WAR CHIEF

(*Angrily.*)
The councils of men are not the place for women.

RED CLOUD

(*Gently.*)
As men grow kind and wise there will be women in the councils of men. As men grow their women must grow with them if they would continue to be the mothers of men.

WAR CHIEF

It is told of old time that there are women in the councils of the Sun. And is it not told that the Sun Man will destroy us?

RED CLOUD

Then is the Sun Man the stronger; it may be because of his kindness and wiseness, and because of his women.

YOUNG BRAVE

Is it told that the women of the Sun are good to the eye, soft to the arm, and a fire in the heart of man?

SHAMAN

(*Holding up hand solemnly.*)
It were well, lest the young do not forget, to repeat the old word again.

WAR CHIEF

(*Nodding confirmation.*)
Here, where the tale is told.
(*Pointing to the spring.*)
Here, where the water burst from under the heel of the Sun Man mounting into the sky.
(WAR CHIEF *leads the way up the hillside to the spring, and signals to the* OLD MAN *to begin.*)

THE SNARING OF THE SUN

OLD MAN

When the world was in the making,
Here within the mighty forest,
Came the Sun Man every morning.
White and shining was the Sun Man,
Blue his eyes were as the sky-blue,
Bright his hair was as dry grass is,
Warm his eyes were as the sun is,
Fruit and flower were in his glances ;
All he looked on grew and sprouted,
As these trees we see about us,
Mightiest trees in all the forest,
For the Sun Man looked upon them.
Where his glance fell grasses seeded,
Where his feet fell sprang up starting —
Buckeye woods and hazel thickets,
Berry bushes, manzanita,
Till his pathway was a garden,
Flowing after like a river,
Laughing into bud and blossom.

There was never frost nor famine
And the Nishinam were happy,

Singing, dancing through the seasons,
Never cold and never hungered,
When the Sun Man lived among us.

But the foxes mean and cunning,
Hating Nishinam and all men,
Laid their snares within this forest,
Caught the Sun Man in the morning,
With their ropes of sinew caught him,
Bound him down to steal his wisdom
And become themselves bright Sun Men,
Warm of glance and fruitful-footed,
Masters of the frost and famine.

Swiftly the Coyote running
Came to aid the fallen Sun Man,
Swiftly killed the cunning foxes,
Swiftly cut the ropes of sinew,
Swiftly the Coyote freed him.

But the Sun Man in his anger,
Lightning flashing, thunder-throwing,
Loosed the frost and fanged the famine,
Thorned the bushes, pinched the berries,
Put the bitter in the buckeye,
Rocked the mountains to their summits,
Flung the hills into the valleys,
Sank the lakes and shoaled the rivers,
Poured the fresh sea in the salt sea,
Stamped his foot here in the forest,
Where the water burst from under
Heel that raised him into heaven —
Angry with the world forever
Rose the Sun Man into heaven.

SHAMAN

(*Solemnly.*)
I am the Shaman. I know what has gone before and what will come after. I have passed down through the gateway of death and talked with the dead. My eyes have looked upon the unseen things. My ears have heard the unspoken words. And now I shall tell you of the Sun Man in the days to come.

(SHAMAN *stiffens suddenly with hideous facial distortions, with inturned eye-balls and loosened jaw. He waves his arms about, writhes and twists in torment, as if in epilepsy.*)

(*The* WOMEN *break into a wailing, inarticulate chant, swaying their bodies to the accent. The men join them somewhat reluctantly, all save* RED CLOUD, *who betrays vexation, and* WAR CHIEF, *who betrays truculence.*)

(SHAMAN, *leading the rising frenzy, with convulsive shiverings and tremblings tears off his skin garments so that he is quite naked save for a girdle of eagle-claws about his thighs. His long black hair flies about his face. With an abruptness that is startling, he ceases all movement and stands erect, rigid. This is greeted with a low moaning that slowly dies away.*)

CHANT OF PROPHECY

SHAMAN

The Sun never grows cold.
The Sun Man is like the Sun.
His anger never grows cold.
The Sun Man will return.
The Sun Man will come back from the Sun.

PEOPLE

The Sun Man will return.
The Sun Man will come back from the Sun.

SHAMAN

There is a sign.
As the water burst forth when he rose into the sky,
So will the water cease to flow when he returns from the sky.
The Sun Man is mighty.
In his eyes is blue fire.
In his hands he bears the thunder.
The lightnings are in his hair.

People

In his hands he bears the thunder.
The lightnings are in his hair.

Shaman

There is a sign.
The Sun Man is white.
His skin is white like the sun.
His hair is bright like the sunlight.
His eyes are blue like the sky.

People

There is a sign.
The Sun Man is white.

Shaman

The Sun Man is mighty.
He is the enemy of the Nishinam.
He will destroy the Nishinam.

People

He is the enemy of the Nishinam.
He will destroy the Nishinam.

Shaman

There is a sign.
The Sun Man will bear the thunder in his hand.

People

There is a sign.
The Sun Man will bear the thunder in his hand.

Shaman

In the day the Sun Man comes
The water from the spring will no longer flow.
And in that day he will destroy the Nishinam.

With the thunder will he destroy the Nishinam.
The Nishinam will be like last year's grasses.
The Nishinam will be like the smoke of last year's campfires.
The Nishinam will be less than the dreams that trouble
the sleeper.
The Nishinam will be like the days no man remembers.
I am the Shaman.
I have spoken.

>*(The* PEOPLE *set up a sad wailing.)*

WAR CHIEF

>*(Striking his chest with his fist.)*

Hoh ! Hoh ! Hoh !

>*(The* PEOPLE *cease from their wailing and look to the* WAR CHIEF *with hopeful expectancy.)*

WAR CHIEF

I am the War Chief. In war I command. Nor the Shaman nor Red Cloud may say me nay when in war I command. Let the Sun Man come back. I am not afraid. If the foxes snared him with ropes, then can I slay him with spear-thrust and war-club. I am the War Chief. In war I command.

>*(The* PEOPLE *greet* WAR CHIEF'S *pronouncement with warlike cries of approval.)*

RED CLOUD

The foxes are cunning. If they snared the Sun Man with ropes of sinew, then let us be cunning and snare him with ropes of kindness. In kindness, O War Chief, is strength, much strength.

SHAMAN

Red Cloud speaks true. In kindness is strength.

WAR CHIEF

I am the War Chief.

SHAMAN

You cannot slay the Sun Man.

WAR CHIEF

I am the War Chief.

SHAMAN

The Sun Man fights with the thunder in his hand.

WAR CHIEF

I am the War Chief.

RED CLOUD

(*As he speaks the* PEOPLE *are visibly won by his argument.*)

You speak true, O War Chief. In war you command. You are strong, most strong. You have slain the Modoc. You have slain the Napa. You have slain the Clam-Eaters of the big water till the last one is not. Yet you have not slain all the foxes. The foxes cannot fight, yet are they stronger than you because you cannot slay them. The foxes are foxes, but we are men. When the Sun Man comes we will not be cunning like the foxes. We will be kind. Kindness and love will we give to the Sun Man, so that he will be our friend. Then will he melt the frost, pull the teeth of famine, give us back our rivers of deep water, our lakes of sweet water, take the bitter from the buckeye, and in all ways make the world the good world it was before he left us.

PEOPLE

Hail, Red Cloud, the first man!
Hail, Red Cloud, the Acorn-Planter!
Who showed us the way of our feet in the world!
Who showed us the way of our food in the world!
Who showed us the way of our hearts in the world!
Who gave us the law of family,
The law of tribe,
The law of totem,
And made us strong in the world among men!

(*While the* PEOPLE *sing the hillside slowly grows dark.*)

ACT I

(Ten thousand years have passed, and it is the time of the early voyaging from Europe to the waters of the Pacific, when the deserted hillside is again revealed as the moon rises. The stream no longer flows from the spring. Since the grove is used only as a camp for the night when the Nishinam are on their seasonal migration, there are no signs of previous camps.)

(Enter from right, at end of day's march, women, old men, and SHAMAN, *the women bending under their burdens of camp gear and dunnage.)*

(Enter from left youths carrying fish-spears and large fish.)

(Appear, coming down the hillside, RED CLOUD *and the hunters, many carrying meat.)*

(The various repeated characters, despite differences of skin garmenting and decoration, resemble their prototypes of the prologue.)

RED CLOUD

Good hunting ! Good hunting !

HUNTERS

Good hunting ! Good hunting !

YOUTHS

Good fishing ! Good fishing !

WOMEN

Good berries ! Good acorns !

(The women and youths and hunters, as they reach the camp-site, begin throwing down their burdens.)

Dew-Woman

(*Discovering the dry spring.*)
The water no longer flows!

Shaman

(*Stilling the excitement that is immediate on the discovery.*)
The word of old time that has come down to us from all the Shamans who have gone before! The Sun Man has come back from the Sun.

Dew-Woman

(*Looking to* Red Cloud.)
Let Red Cloud speak. Since the morning of the world has Red Cloud ever been reborn with the ancient wisdom to guide us.

War Chief

Save in war. In war I command.
(*He picks out hunters by name.*)
Deer Foot . . . Elk Man . . . Antelope. Run through the forest, climb the hill-tops, seek down the valleys, for aught you may find of this Sun Man.
(*At a wave of the* War Chief's *hand the three hunters depart in different directions.*)

Dew-Woman

Let Red Cloud speak his mind.

Red Cloud

(*Quietly.*)
Last night the earth shook and there was a roaring in the air. Often have I seen, when the earth shakes and there is a roaring, that springs in some places dry up, and that in other places where were no springs, springs burst forth.

SHAMAN

There is a sign.
The Shamans told it of old.
The Sun Man will bear the thunder in his hand.

PEOPLE

There is a sign.
The Sun Man will bear the thunder in his hand.

SHAMAN

The roaring in the air was the thunder of the Sun Man's return. Now will he destroy the Nishinam. Such is the word.

WAR CHIEF

Hoh ! Hoh !
(*From right* DEER FOOT *runs in.*)

DEER FOOT

(*Breathless.*)
They come ! He comes !

WAR CHIEF

Who comes?

DEER FOOT

The Sun Men. The Sun Man. He is their chief. He marches before them. And he is white.

PEOPLE

There is a sign.
The Sun Man is white.

Red Cloud

Carries he the thunder in his hand ?

Deer Foot

(*Puzzled.*)
He looks hungry.

War Chief

Hoh ! Hoh ! The Sun Man is hungry. It will be easy to kill a hungry Sun Man.

Red Cloud

It would be easy to be kind to a hungry Sun Man and give him food. We have much. The hunting has been good.

War Chief

Better to kill the Sun Man.
(*He turns upon* People, *indicating most commands in gestures as he prepares the ambush, making women and boys conceal all the camp outfit and game, and disposing the armed hunters among the ferns and behind trees till all are hidden.*)

Elk Man and Antelope

(*Running down hillside.*)
The Sun Man comes.

(War Chief *sends them to hiding places.*)

War Chief

(*Preparing himself to hide.*)
You have not hidden, O Red Cloud.

Red Cloud

(*Stepping into shadow of big tree where he remains*

inconspicuous though dimly visible.)
I would see this Sun Man and talk with him.
> *(The sound of singing is heard, and* WAR CHIEF *conceals himself.)*
>
> (SUN MAN, *with handful of followers, singing to ease the tedium of the march, enter from right. They are patently survivors of a wrecked exploring ship, making their way inland.)*

SONG OF THE SEA CUNIES

SUN MEN

We sailed three hundred strong
   For the far Barbaree ;
Our voyage has been most long
   For the far Barbaree ;
     So—it's a long pull,
     Give a strong pull,
   For the far Barbaree.

We sailed the oceans wide
   For the coast of Barbaree ;
And left our ship a sinking
   On the coast of Barbaree ;
     So—it's a long pull,
     Give a strong pull,
   For the far Barbaree.

Our ship went fast a-lee
   On the rocks of Barbaree ;
That's why we quit the sea
   On the rocks of Barbaree.
     So—it's a long pull,
     Give a strong pull,
   For the far Barbaree.

We quit the bitter seas
   On the coast of Barbaree ;
To seek the savag-ees
   Of the far Barbaree.
     So—it's a long pull,

Give a strong pull,
　　　　For the far Barbaree.
Our feet are lame and sore
　　In the far Barbaree;
From treading of the shore
　　Of the far Barbaree.
　　　So—it's a long pull,
　　　Give a strong pull,
　　　For the far Barbaree.

A weary brood are we
　　In the far Barbaree;
Sea cunies of the sea
　　In the far Barbaree.
　　　So—it's a long pull,
　　　Give a strong pull,
　　　For the far Barbaree.

SUN MAN

(*Who alone carries a musket, and who is evidently captain of the wrecked company.*)
No farther can we go this night. Mayhap to-morrow we may find the savages and food.
(*He glances about.*)
This far world grows noble trees. We shall sleep as in a temple.

FIRST SEA CUNY

(*Espying* RED CLOUD, *and pointing.*)
Look, Captain!

SUN MAN

(*Making the universal peace-sign, arm raised and out, palm-outward.*)
Who are you? Speak. We come in peace. We kindness seek.

RED CLOUD

(*Advancing out of the shadow.*)
Whence do you come?

SUN MAN

From the great sea.

RED CLOUD

I do not understand. No one journeys on the great sea.

SUN MAN

We have journeyed many moons.

RED CLOUD

Have you come from the sun ?

SUN MAN

God wot ! We have journeyed across the sun, high and low in the sky, and over the sun and under the sun the round world 'round.

RED CLOUD

(*With conviction.*)
You come from the Sun. Your hair is like the summer sunburnt grasses. Your eyes are blue. Your skin is white.
(*With absolute conviction.*)
You are the Sun Man.

SUN MAN

(*With a shrug of shoulders.*)
Have it so. I come from the Sun. I am the Sun Man.

RED CLOUD

Do you carry the thunder in your hand?

SUN MAN

(*Nonplussed for the moment, glances at his musket, then smiles.*)

Yes, I carry the thunder in my hand.

> (WAR CHIEF *and the* HUNTERS *leap suddenly from ambush.* SUN MAN *warns* SEA CUNIES *not to resist.* WAR CHIEF *captures and holds* SUN MAN, *and* SEA CUNIES *are similarly captured and held. Women and boys appear, and examine prisoners curiously.*)

WAR CHIEF

Hoh ! Hoh ! Hoh ! I have captured the Sun Man ! Like the foxes, I have captured the Sun Man !—Deer Foot ! Elk Man ! The foxes held the Sun Man. I now hold the Sun Man. Then can you hold the Sun Man.

> (DEER FOOT *and* ELK MAN *seize the* SUN MAN.)

RED CLOUD

(*To* SHAMAN.)
He said he came in kindness.

WAR CHIEF

(*Sneering.*)
In kindness, with the thunder in his hand.

SHAMAN

> (*Deflected to partisanship of* WAR CHIEF *by* WAR CHIEF'S *success.*)

By his own lips has he said it, with the thunder in his hand.

WAR CHIEF

You are the Sun Man.

SUN MAN

(*Shrugging shoulders.*)
My names are many as the stars. Call me White Man.

RED CLOUD

I am Red Cloud, the first man.

SUN MAN

Then am I Adam, the first man and your brother.
(Glancing about.)
And this is Eden, to look upon it.

RED CLOUD

My father was the Coyote.

SUN MAN

My father was Jehovah.

RED CLOUD

I am the Fire-Bringer. I stole the fire from the ground squirrel and hid it in the heart of the wood.

SUN MAN

Then am I Prometheus, your brother. I stole the fire from heaven and hid it in the heart of the wood.

RED CLOUD

I am the Acorn-Planter. I am the Food-Bringer, the Life-Maker. I make food for more life, ever more life.

SUN MAN

Then am I truly your brother. Life-Maker am I, tilling the soil in the sweat of my brow from the beginning of time, planting all manner of good seeds for the harvest.
(Looking sharply at RED CLOUD'S *skin garments.)*
Also am I the Weaver and Cloth-Maker.
(Holding out arm so that RED CLOUD *may examine the cloth of the coat.)*
From the hair of the goat and the wool of the sheep, and from beaten and spun grasses, do I make the cloth to keep man warm.

SHAMAN

(Breaking in boastfully.)

I am the Shaman. I know all secret things.

SUN MAN

I know my pathway under the sun over all the seas, and I know the secrets of the stars that show me my path where no path is. I know when the Wolf of Darkness shall eat the moon.
> (*Pointing toward moon.*)

On this night shall the Wolf of Darkness eat the moon.
> (*He turns suddenly to* RED CLOUD, *drawing sheath-knife and passing it to him.*)

More, O First Man and Acorn-Planter. I am the Iron-Maker. Behold!
> (RED CLOUD *examines knife, understands immediately its virtue, cuts easily a strip of skin from his skin garment, and is overcome with the wonder of the knife.*)

WAR CHIEF

> (*Exhibiting a long bow.*)

I am the War Chief. No man, save me, has strength to bend this bow. I can slay farther than any man.
> (*A huge bear has come out among the bushes far up the hillside*)

SUN MAN

I, too, am War Chief over men, and I can slay farther than you.

WAR CHIEF

Hoh! Hoh!

SUN MAN

> (*Pointing to bear.*)

Can you slay that with your strong bow?

WAR CHIEF

(Dubiously.)
It is a far shot. Too far. No man can slay a great bear so far.
> (SUN MAN, *shaking off from his arms the hands of* DEER FOOT *and* ELK MAN, *aims musket and fires. The bear falls, and the Nishinam betray astonishment and awe.*)
> (*At a quick signal from* WAR CHIEF, SUN MAN *is again seized.* WAR CHIEF *takes away musket and examines it.*)

SHAMAN

There is a sign.

PEOPLE

There is a sign.
He carries the thunder in his hand.
He slays with the thunder in his hand.
He is the enemy of the Nishinam.
He will destroy the Nishinam.

SHAMAN

There is a sign.

PEOPLE

There is a sign.
In the day the Sun Man comes,
The waters from the spring will no longer flow,
And in that day will he destroy the Nishinam.

WAR CHIEF

(Exhibiting musket.)
Hoh! Hoh! I have taken the Sun Man's thunder.

SHAMAN

Now shall the Sun Man die that the Nishinam may live.

RED CLOUD

He is our brother. He, too, is an acorn-planter. He has spoken.

SHAMAN

He is the Sun Man, and he is our eternal enemy. He shall die.

WAR CHIEF

In war I command.
   (*To* HUNTERS.)
Tie their feet with stout thongs that they may not run.
And then make ready with bow and arrow to do the deed.
   (HUNTERS *obey, urging and thrusting the* SEA CUNIES
      into a compact group behind the SUN MAN.)

RED CLOUD

Shaman I am not.
I know not the secret things.
I say the things I know.
When you plant kindness you harvest kindness.
When you plant blood you harvest blood.
He who plants one acorn makes way for life.
He who slays one man slays the planter of a thousand acorns.

SHAMAN

Shaman I am.
I see the dark future.
I see the Sun Man's death,
The journey he must take
Through thick and endless forest
Where lost souls wander howling
A thousand moons of moons.

PEOPLE

Through thick and endless forest
Where lost souls wander howling
A thousand moons of moons.

> (WAR CHIEF *arranges* HUNTERS *with their bows and arrows for the killing.*)

SUN MAN

(*To* RED CLOUD.)
You will slay us ?

RED CLOUD

(*Indicating* WAR CHIEF.)
In war he commands.

SUN MAN

(*Addressing the Nishinam*)
Nor am I a Shaman. But I will tell you true things to be. Our brothers are acorn-planters, cloth-weavers, iron-workers. Our brothers are life-makers and masters of life. Many are our brothers and strong. They will come after us. Your First Man has spoken true words. When you plant blood you harvest blood. Our brothers will come to the harvest with the thunder in their hands. There is a sign. This night, and soon, will the Wolf of Darkness eat the moon. And by that sign will our brothers come on the trail we have broken.

> (*As final preparation for the killing is completed, and as* HUNTERS *are arranged with their bows and arrows,* SUN MAN *sings.*)

SONG OF THE BROTHERS

SUN MAN

Our brothers will come after,
   On our trail to farthest lands ;
Our brothers will come after
   With the thunder in their hands.

Sun Men

Loud will be the weeping,
Red will be the reaping,
High will be the heaping
Of the slain their law commands.

Sun Man

Givers of law, our brothers,
    This is the law they say :
Who takes the life of a brother
    Ten of the slayers shall pay.

Sun Men

Our brothers will come after,
    On our trail to farthest lands ;
Our brothers will come after
    With the thunder in their hands.
    Loud will be the weeping,
    Red will be the reaping,
    High will be the heaping
Of the slain their law commands.

Sun Man

Our brothers will come after
    By the courses that we lay ;
Many and strong our brothers,
    Masters of life are they.

Sun Men

Our brothers will come after
    On our trail to farthest lands ;
Our brothers will come after
    With the thunder in their hands.
    Loud will be the weeping,
    Red will be the reaping,
    High will be the heaping
Of the slain their law commands.

SUN MAN

Plowers of land, our brothers,
    Of the hills and pleasant leas;
Under the sun our brothers
    With their keels will plow the seas.

SUN MEN

Our brothers will come after,
    On our trail to farthest lands ;
Our brothers will come after
    With the thunder in their hands.
        Loud will be the weeping,
        Red will be the reaping,
        High will be the heaping
Of the slain their law commands.

SUN MAN

Mighty men are our brothers,
    Quick to forgive and to wrath,
Sailing the seas, our brothers
    Will follow us on our path.

SUN MEN

Our brothers will come after,
    On our trail to farthest lands;
Our brothers will come after
    With the thunder in their hands.
        Loud will be the weeping,
        Red will be the reaping,
        High will be the heaping
Of the slain their law commands.

(At signal from WAR CHIEF *the arrows are discharged, and repeatedly discharged. The* SUN MAN *fall. The* WAR CHIEF *himself kills the* SUN MAN.*)*

(In what follows, RED CLOUD *and* DEW-WOMAN *stand aside, taking no part.* RED CLOUD *is depressed, and at the same time is overcome with the wonder of the knife which he still holds.)*

WAR CHIEF

(Brandishing musket and drifting stiff-legged as he sings, into the beginning of a war dance of victory.)

Hoh ! Hoh ! Hoh !
I have slain the Sun Man !
Hoh ! Hoh ! Hoh !
I hold his thunder in my hand !
Hoh ! Hoh ! Hoh !
Greatest of War Chiefs am I !
Hoh ! Hoh ! Hoh !
I have slain the Sun Man !

(The dance grows wilder.)
(After a time the hillside begins to darken.)

DEW-WOMAN

(Pointing to the moon entering eclipse.)
Lo ! The Wolf of Darkness eats the Moon !

(In consternation the dance is broken off for the moment.)

SHAMAN

(Reassuringly.)
It is a sign.
The Sun Man is dead.

WAR CHIEF

(Recovering courage and resuming dance.)
Hoh ! Hoh ! Hoh !
The Sun Man is dead!

PEOPLE

(Resuming dance.)
Hoh ! Hoh ! Hoh !
The Sun Man is dead!

(As darkness increases the dance grows into a saturnalia, until complete darkness settles down and hides the hillside.)

ACT II

(A hundred years have passed, when the hillside and the Nishinam in their temporary camp are revealed. The spring is flowing, and Women are filling gourds with water. RED CLOUD *and* DEW-WOMAN *stand apart from their people.)*

SHAMAN

(Pointing.)
There is a sign.
The spring lives.
The water flows from the spring
And all is well with the Nishinam.

PEOPLE

There is a sign.
The spring lives.
The water flows from the spring.

WAR CHIEF

(Boastingly.)
Hoh! Hoh! Hoh!
All is well with the Nishinam.
Hoh! Hoh! Hoh!
It is I who have made all well with the Nishinam.
Hoh! Hoh! Hoh!
I led our young men against the Napa.
Hoh! Hoh! Hoh!
We left no man living of the camp.
Hoh! Hoh! Hoh!

SHAMAN

Great is our War Chief!
Good is war!
No more will the Napa hunt our meat.
No more will the Napa pick our berries.
No more will the Napa catch our fish.

People

No more will the Napa hunt our meat
No more will the Napa pick our berries.
No more will the Napa catch our fish.

War Chief

Hoh ! Hoh ! Hoh !
The War Chiefs before me made all well with the Nishinam.
Hoh ! Hoh ! Hoh !
The War Chief of long ago slew the Sun Man.
Hoh ! Hoh ! Hoh !
The Sun Man said his brothers would come after.
Hoh ! Hoh ! Hoh !
The Sun Man lied.

People

Hoh ! Hoh ! Hoh !
The Sun Man lied.
Hoh ! Hoh ! Hoh !
The Sun Man lied.

Shaman

(*Derisively.*)
Red Cloud is sick. He lives in dreams. Ever he dreams of the wonders of the Sun Man.

Red Cloud

The Sun Man was strong. The Sun Man was a life-maker. The Sun Man planted acorns, and cut quickly with a knife not of bone nor stone, and of grasses and hides made cunning cloth that is better than all grasses and hides.—Old Man, where is the cunning cloth that is better than all grasses and hides ?

Old Man

(*Fumbling in his skin pouch for the cloth.*)
In the many moons aforetime,
Hundred moons and many hundred,
When the old man was the young man,
When the young man was the youngling,
Dragging branches for the campfire,
Stealing suet from the bear-meat,
Cause of trouble to his mother,
Came the Sun Man in the night-time.
I alone of all the Nishinam
Live to-day to tell the story ;
I alone of all the Nishinam
Saw the Sun Man come among us,
Heard the Sun Man and his Sun Men
Sing their death-song here among us
Ere they died beneath our arrows,
War Chief's arrows sharp and feathered—

WAR CHIEF

(*Interrupting braggartly.*)
Hoh ! Hoh ! Hoh !

OLD MAN

(*Producing cloth.*)
And the Sun Man and his Sun Men
Wore nor hair nor hide nor birdskin.
Cloth they wore from beaten grasses
Woven like our willow baskets,
Willow-woven acorn baskets
Women make in acorn season.

(OLD MAN *hands piece of cloth to* RED CLOUD.)

RED CLOUD

(*Admiring cloth.*)
The Sun Man was an acorn-planter, and we killed the Sun Man. We were not kind. We made a blood-debt. Blood-debts are not good.

SHAMAN

The Sun Man lied. His brothers did not come after. There is no blood-debt when there is no one to make us pay.

RED CLOUD

He who plants acorns reaps food, and food is life. He who sows war reaps war, and war is death.

PEOPLE

(*Encouraged by* SHAMAN *and* WAR CHIEF *to drown out* RED CLOUD'S *voice.*)
Hoh ! Hoh ! Hoh !
The Sun Man is dead !
Hoh ! Hoh ! Hoh !
The Sun Man and his Sun Men are dead !

RED CLOUD

(*Shaking his head.*)
His brothers of the Sun are coming after. I have reports.

(RED CLOUD *beckons one after another of the young hunters to speak.*)

FIRST HUNTER

To the south, not far, I wandered and lived with the Petaluma. With my eyes I did not see, but it was told me by those whose eyes had seen, that still to the south, not far, were many Sun Men—war chiefs who carry the thunder in their hands ; cloth-makers and weavers of cloth like to that in Red Cloud's hand ; acorn-planters who plant all manner of strange seeds that ripen to rich harvests of food that is good. And there had been trouble. The Petaluma had killed Sun Men, and many Petaluma had the Sun Men killed.

SECOND HUNTER

To the east, not far, I wandered and lived with the Solano.

With my own eyes I did not see, but it was told me by those whose eyes had seen, that still to the east, not far, and just beyond the lands of the Tule tribes, were many Sun Men—war chiefs and cloth-makers and acorn-planters. And there had been trouble. The Solano had killed Sun Men, and many Solano had the Sun Men killed.

THIRD HUNTER

To the north, and far, I wandered and lived with the Klamath. With my own eyes I did not see, but it was told me by those whose eyes had seen, that still to the north, and far, were many Sun Men—war chiefs and cloth-makers and acorn-planters. And there had been trouble. The Klamath had killed Sun Men, and many Klamath had the Sun Men killed.

FOURTH HUNTER

To the west, not far, three days gone I wandered, where, from the mountain, I looked down upon the great sea. With my own eyes I saw. It was like a great bird that swam upon the water. It had great wings like to our great trees here. And on its back I saw men, many men, and they were Sun Men. With my own eyes I saw.

RED CLOUD

We shall be kind to the Sun Men when they come among us.

WAR CHIEF

(*Dancing stiff-legged.*)
Hoh ! Hoh ! Hoh !
Let the Sun Men come!
Hoh ! Hoh ! Hoh !
We will kill the Sun Men when they come!

PEOPLE

(*As they join in the war dance.*)
Hoh ! Hoh ! Hoh !

Let the Sun Men come!
Hoh ! Hoh ! Hoh !
We will kill the Sun Men when they come.

> (*The dance grows wilder, the* SHAMAN *and* WAR CHIEF *encouraging it, while* RED CLOUD *and* DEW-WOMAN *stand sadly at a distance.*)

> (*Rifle shots ring out from every side. Up the hillside appear* SUN MEN *firing rifles. The Nishinam reel to death from their dancing.*)

> (RED CLOUD *shields* DEW-WOMAN *with one arm about her, and with the other arm makes the peace-sign.*)

> (*The massacre is complete,* DEW-WOMAN *and* RED CLOUD *being the last to fall.* RED CLOUD, *wounded, the sole survivor, rests on his elbow and watches the* SUN MEN *assemble about their leader.*)

> (*The* SUN MEN *are the type of pioneer Americans who, even before the discovery of gold, were already drifting across the Sierras and down into Oregon and California with their oxen and great wagons. With here and there a Rocky Mountain trapper or a buckskin-clad scout of the Kit Carson type, in the main they are backwoods farmers. All carry the long rifle of the period.*)

> (*The* SUN MAN *is buckskin-clad, with long blond hair sweeping his shoulders.*)

SUN MEN

(*Led by* SUN MAN.)
We crossed the Western Ocean
   Three hundred years ago,
We cleared New England's forests
   Three hundred years ago.
     Blow high, blow low,
     Heigh hi, heigh ho,

We cleared New England's forests
    Three hundred years ago.
We climbed the Alleghanies
    Two hundred years ago,
We reached the Susquehanna
    Two hundred years ago.
        Blow high, blow low,
        Heigh hi, heigh ho,
We reached the Susquehanna
    Two hundred years ago.

We crossed the Mississippi
    One hundred years ago,
And glimpsed the Rocky Mountains
    One hundred years ago.
        Blow high, blow low,
        Heigh hi, heigh ho,
And glimpsed the Rocky Mountains
    One hundred years ago.

We passed the Rocky Mountains
    A year or so ago,
And crossed the salty deserts
    A year or so ago.
        Blow high, blow low,
        Heigh hi, heigh ho,
And crossed the salty deserts
    A year or so ago.

We topped the high Sierras
    But a few days ago,
And saw great California
    But a few days ago.
        Blow high, blow low,
        Heigh hi, heigh ho,
And saw great California
    But a few days ago.

We crossed Sonoma's mountains
    An hour or so ago,
And found this mighty forest
    An hour or so ago.

Blow high, blow low,
Heigh hi, heigh ho,
And found this mighty forest
An hour or so ago.

SUN MAN

(*Glancing about at the slain and at the giant forest.*)
Good the day, good the deed, and good this California land.

RED CLOUD

Not with these eyes, but with other eyes in my lives before, have I beheld you. You are the Sun Man.

(*The attention of all is drawn to* RED CLOUD, *and they group about him and the* SUN MAN.)

SUN MAN

Call me White Man. Though in truth we follow the sun. All our lives have we followed the sunset sun, as our fathers followed it before us.

RED CLOUD

And you slay us with the thunder in your hand. You slay us because we slew your brothers.

SUN MAN

(*Nodding to* RED CLOUD *and addressing his own followers.*)
You see, it was no mistake. He confesses it. Other white men have they slain.

RED CLOUD

There will come a day when men will not slay men and when all men will be brothers. And in that day all men will plant acorns.

SUN MAN

You speak well, brother.

RED CLOUD

Ever was I for peace, but in war I did not command. Ever I sought the secrets of the growing things, the times and seasons for planting. Ever I planted acorns, making two black oak trees grow where one grew before. And now all is ended. Oh my black oak acorns ! My black oak acorns ! Who will plant them now ?

SUN MAN

Be of good cheer. We, too, are planters. Rich is your land here. Not from poor soil can such trees sprout heavenward. We will plant many seeds and grow mighty harvests.

RED CLOUD

I planted the short acorns in the valley. I planted the long acorns in the valley. I made food for life.

SUN MAN

You planted well, brother, but not well enough. It is for that reason that you pass. Your fat valley grows food but for a handful of men. We shall plant your fat valley and grow food for ten thousand men.

RED CLOUD

Ever I counseled peace and planting.

SUN MAN

Some day all men will counsel peace. No man will slay his fellow. All men will plant.

RED CLOUD

But before that day you will slay, as you have this day slain us?

SUN MAN

You killed our brothers first. Blood-debts must be paid. It is man's way upon the earth. But more, O brother ! We follow the sunset sun, and the way before us is red with war. The way behind us is white with peace. Ever, before us, we make room for life. Ever we slay the squalling crawling things of the wild. Ever we clear the land and destroy the weeds that block the way of life for the seeds we plant. We are many, and many are our brothers that come after along the way of peace we blaze. Where you make two black oaks grow in the place of one, we make an hundred. And where we make one grow, our brothers who come after make an hundred hundred.

RED CLOUD

Truly are you the Sun Man. We knew about you of old time. Our old men knew and sang of you:

>White and shining was the Sun Man,
>Blue his eyes were as the sky-blue,
>Bright his hair was as dry grass is,
>Warm his eyes were as the sun is,
>Fruit and flower were in his glances,
>All he looked on grew and sprouted,
>Where his glance fell grasses seeded,
>Where his feet fell sprang upstarting
>Buckeye woods and hazel thickets,
>Berry bushes, manzanita,
>Till his pathway was a garden,
>Flowing after like a river
>Laughing into bud and blossom.

SONG OF THE PIONEERS

SUN MEN

Our brothers follow on the trail we blaze.
    Where howled the wolf and ached the naked plain
        Spring bounteous harvests at our brothers' hands ;
In place of war's alarums, peaceful days ;
    Above the warrior's grave the golden grain
        Turns deserts grim and stark to laughing lands.

SUN MAN

We cleared New England's flinty slopes and plowed
Her rocky fields to fairness in the sun,
But fared we westward always for we sought
A land of golden richness and we knew
The land was waiting on the sunset trail.
Where we found forest we left fertile fields,
We bridled rivers wild to grind our corn,
The deer-paths turned to roadways at our heels,
Our axes felled the trees that bridged the streams,
And fenced the meadow pastures for our kine.

SUN MEN

Our brothers follow on the trail we blaze ;
    Where howled the wolf and ached the naked plain
        Spring bounteous harvests at our brothers' hands;
In place of war's alarums, peaceful days ;
    Above the warrior's grave the golden grain
        Turns deserts grim and stark to laughing lands.

SUN MAN

Beyond the Mississippi still we fared,
And rested weary by the River Platte
Until the young grass velveted the Plains,
Then yoked again our oxen to the trail
That ever led us west to farthest west.
Our women toiled beside us, and our young,
And helped to break the soil and plant the corn,
And fought beside us in the battle front
To fight of arrow, whine of bullet, when
We chained our circled wagons wheel to wheel.

SUN MEN

Our brothers follow on the trail we blaze;
    Where howled the wolf and ached the naked plain
        Spring bounteous harvests at our brothers' hands ;
In place of war's alarums, peaceful days ;
    Above the warrior's grave the golden grain
        Turns deserts grim and stark to laughing lands.

SUN MAN

The rivers sank beneath the desert sand,
The tall pines dwarfed to sage-brush, and the grass
Grew sparse and bitter in the alkali,
But fared we always toward the setting sun.
Our oxen famished till the last one died
And our great wagons rested in the snow.
We climbed the high Sierras and looked down
From winter bleak upon the land we sought,
A sunny land, a rich and fruitful land,
The warm and golden California land.

SUN MEN

Our brothers follow on the trail we blaze ;
    Where howled the wolf and ached the naked plain
        Spring bounteous harvests at our brothers' hands ;
In place of war's alarums, peaceful days ;
    Above the warrior's grave the golden grain
        Turns deserts grim and stark to laughing lands.

(*The hillside begins to darken.*)

RED CLOUD

(*Faintly.*)
The darkness is upon me. You are acorn-planters. You are my brothers. The darkness is upon me and I pass.

SUN MEN

(*As total darkness descends*)
Our brothers follow on the trail we blaze ;
    Where howled the wolf and ached the naked plain
        Spring bounteous harvests at our brothers' hands ;
In place of war's alarums, peaceful days ;
    Above the warrior's grave the golden grain
        Turns deserts grim and stark to laughing lands.

EPILOGUE

RED CLOUD

Good tidings ! Good tidings
To the sons of men !
Good tidings ! Good tidings !
War is dead !

> (*Light begins to suffuse the hillside, revealing* RED
> CLOUD *far up the hillside in a commanding position
> on an out-jut of rock.*)

Lo, the New Day dawns,
The day of brotherhood,
The day when all men
Shall be kind to all men,
And all men shall be sowers of life.

> (*From every side a burst of voices.*)

Hail to Red Cloud !
The Acorn-Planter !
The Life-Maker !
Hail ! All hail !
The New Day dawns,
The day of brotherhood,
The day of man.

> (*A band of* WARRIORS *appears on hillside.*)

WARRIORS

Hail, Red Cloud !
Mightier than all fighting men !
The slayer of War!
We are not sad.
Our eyes were blinded.
We did not know one acorn planted
Was mightier than an hundred fighting men.
We are not sad.
Our red work was when

The world was young and wild.
The world has grown wise.
No man slays his brother.
Our work is done.
In the light of the new day are we glad.

(A band of PIONEERS *and* SEA EXPLORERS *appears.)*

PIONEERS and EXPLORERS

Hail, Red Cloud !
The first planter !
The Acorn-Planter !
We sang that War would die,
The anarch of our wild and wayward past.
We sang our brothers would come after,
Turning desert into garden,
Sowing friendship, and not hatred,
Planting seeds instead of dead men,
Growing men to manhood in the sun.

(A band of HUSBANDMEN *appear, bearing fruit and sheaves of grain and corn.)*

HUSBANDMEN

Hail, Red Cloud !
The first planter !
The Acorn-Planter !
The harvests no more are red, but golden.
We are thy children.
We plant for increase,
Increase of wheat and corn,
Of fruit and flower,
Of sheep and kine,
Of love and lovers ;
Rich are our harvests
And many are our lovers.

RED CLOUD

Death is a stench in the nostrils,
Life is beauty and joy.
The planters are ever brothers.
Never are the warriors brothers ;
Their ways are set apart,
Their hands raised each against each.
The planters' ways are the one way.
Ever they plant for life,
For life more abundant,
For beauty of head and hand,
For the voices of children playing,
And the laughter of maids in the twilight
And the lover's song in the gloom.

ALL VOICES

Hail, Red Cloud !
The first planter !
The Acorn-Planter !
The maker of life !
Hail ! All hail !
The New Day dawns,
The day of brotherhood,
The day of man !

THE END

Jack London (R) with George Sterling (L), James Hopper (Sitting), Harry Leon Wilson (Standing at back), Bohemian Grove, 1913

SECTION F

PLAY

THE FIRST POET

This one act play is taken from London's book *The Turtles of Tasman* which was published in September 1916. It was first published in Century Magazine in June 1911. The play was actually written by George Sterling who could not get it published. In a November 16, 1910 letter to Sterling, London declines Sterling's request to publish it under his own name and offers, instead, to make minor revisions and thereby collaborate on it. Obviously, he later relented, possibly because its theme resonated with him as described below. This was the last book published before London's death.

The play underscores London's poetic renascence that began in 1915. Although the play contains only one often reiterated verse, it seems to encapsulate London's inner conflict between writing marketable fiction to put food on the table (in the person of the hunter Uk) and his passion for poetry he could not sell as embodied by "The First Poet" Oan.

It is included in this collection consistent with the inclusion of poetry written by others that London inserted in his own writings. It is a dramatic illustration of London's love of and passion for poetry and how it influenced his own work. In the aforementioned letter, London states that he "be damnably proud to have written" *The First Poet* probably because it so clearly expresses his own beliefs.

THE FIRST POET

SCENE: *A summer plain, the eastern side of which is bounded by grassy hills of limestone, the other sides by a forest. The hill nearest to the plain terminates in a cliff, in the face of which, nearly at the level of the ground, are four caves, with low, narrow entrances. Before the caves, and distant from them less than one hundred feet, is a broad, flat rock, on which are laid several sharp slivers of flint, which, like the rock, are blood-stained. Between the rock and the cave-entrances, on a low pile of stones, is squatted a man, stout and hairy. Across his knees is a thick club, and behind him crouches a woman. At his right and left are two men somewhat resembling him, and like him, bearing wooden clubs. These four face the west, and between them and the bloody rock squat some threescore of cave-folk, talking loudly among themselves. It is late afternoon. The name of him on the pile of stones is Uk, the name of his mate, Ala; and of those at his right and left, Ok and Un.*

UK:

Be still !

(*Turning to the woman behind him*)

Thou seest that they become still. None save me can make his kind be still, except perhaps the chief of the apes, when in the night he deems he hears a serpent. . . . At whom dost thou stare so long ? At OAN ? OAN, come to me !

OAN:

I am thy cub.

UK:

OAN, thou art a fool !

OK AND UN:

Ho ! ho ! OAN is a fool !

ALL THE TRIBE:

Ho ! ho ! OAN is a fool !

OAN:

Why am I a fool ?

UK:

Dost thou not chant strange words ? Last night I heard thee chant strange words at the mouth of thy cave.

OAN:

Ay ! they are marvellous words; they were born within me in the dark.

UK:

Art thou a woman, that thou shouldst bring forth ? Why dost thou not sleep when it is dark ?

OAN:

I did half sleep; perhaps I dreamed.

UK:

And why shouldst thou dream, not having had more than thy portion of flesh ? Hast thou slain a deer in the forest and brought it not to the Stone ?

ALL THE TRIBE:

Wa ! Wa ! He hath slain in the forest, and brought not the meat to the Stone !

UK:

Be still, ye !

(To ALA)

Thou seest that they become still. . . . Oan, hast thou slain and kept to thyself ?

OAN:

Nay, thou knowest that I am not apt at the chase. Also it irks me to squat on a branch all day above a path, bearing a rock upon my thighs. Those words did but awaken within me when I was peaceless in the night.

UK:

And why wast thou peaceless in the night ?

OAN:

Thy mate wept, for that thou didst beat her.

UK:

Ay ! she lamented loudly. But thou shalt make thy half-sleep henceforth at the mouth of the cave, so that when Gurr the tiger cometh, thou shalt hear him sniff between the boulders, and shalt strike the flints, whose stare he hatest. Gurr cometh nightly to the caves.

ONE OF THE TRIBE:

Ay ! Gurr smelleth the Stone !

UK:

Be still !

(To ALA)

Had he not become still, **OK** and **UN** would have beaten him with their clubs. . . But, Oan, tell us those words that were born to thee when ALA did weep.

OAN (*arising*):

They are wonderful words. They are such:

The bright day is gone —

UK:

Now I see thou art liar as well as fool: behold, the day is not gone !

OAN:

But the day was gone in that hour when my song was born to me.

UK:

Then shouldst thou have sung it only at that time, and not when it is yet day. But beware lest thou awaken me in the night. Make thou many stars, that they fly in the whiskers of Gurr.

OAN:

My song is even of stars.

UK:

It was UL, thy father's wont, ere I slew him with four great stones, to climb to the tops of the tallest trees and reach forth his hand, to see if he might not pluck a star. But I said: "Perhaps they be as chestnut-burs." And all the tribe did laugh. UL was also a fool. But what dost thou sing of stars ?

OAN:

I will begin again:
    The bright day is gone.
    The night maketh me sad, sad, sad —

UK:

Nay, the night maketh thee sad; not sad, sad, sad. For when I say to Ala, "Gather thou dried leaves," I say not, "Gather thou dried leaves, leaves, leaves." Thou art a fool!

OK AND UN:

Thou art a fool!

ALL THE TRIBE:

Thou art a fool!

UK:

Yea, he is a fool. But say on, **OAN**, and tell us of thy chestnut-burs.

OAN:

I will begin again:

> The bright day is gone —

UK:

Thou dost not say, "gone, gone, gone!"

OAN:

I am thy cub. Suffer that I speak: so shall the tribe admire greatly.

UK:

Speak on!

OAN:

I will begin once more:

The bright day is gone.
The night maketh me sad, sad—

UK:

Said I not that "sad" should be spoken but once ? Shall I set OK and UN upon thee with their branches ?

OAN:

But it was so born within me — even "sad, sad —"

UK:

If again thou twice or thrice say "sad," thou shalt be dragged to the Stone.

OAN:

Ow ! Ow ! I am thy cub! Yet listen:

The bright day is gone.
The night maketh me sad —

Ow ! Ow ! thou makest me more sad than the night doth ! The song —

UK:

Ok ! Un ! Be prepared !

OAN (*hastily*):

Nay ! have mercy ! I will begin afresh:

The bright day is gone.
The night maketh me sad.
The — the — the —

UK:

Thou hast forgotten, and art a fool ! See, Ala, he is a fool !

OK AND UN:

He is a fool !

ALL THE TRIBE:

He is a fool !

OAN:

I am not a fool ! This is a new thing. In the past, when ye did chant, O men, ye did leap about the Stone, beating your breasts and crying, "Hai, hai, hai !" Or, if the moon was great, "Hai, hai ! hai, hai, hai !" But this song is made even with such words as ye do speak, and is a great wonder. One may sit at the cave's mouth, and moan it many times as the light goeth out of the sky.

ONE OF THE TRIBE:

Ay ! even thus doth he sit at the mouth of our cave, making us marvel, and more especially the women.

UK:

Be still ! . . . When I would make women marvel, I do show them a wolf's brains upon my club, or the great stone that I cast, or perhaps do whirl my arms mightily, or bring home much meat. How should a man do otherwise ? I will have no songs in this place.

OAN:

Yet suffer that I sing my song unto the tribe. Such things have not been before. It may be that they shall praise thee, seeing that I who do make this song am thy cub.

UK:

Well, let us have the song.

OAN (*facing the tribe*):

The bright day is gone.
The night maketh me sa — sad.
But the stars are very white.
They whisper that the day shall return.
O stars; little pieces of the day!

UK:

This is indeed madness. Hast thou heard a star whisper? Did UL, thy father, tell thee that he heard the stars whisper when he was in the tree-top? And of what moment is it that a star be a piece of the day, seeing that its light is of no value? Thou art a fool!

OK AND UN:

Thou art a fool!

ALL THE TRIBE:

Thou art a fool!

OAN:

But it was so born unto me. And at that birth it was as though I would weep, yet had not been stricken; I was moreover glad, yet none had given me a gift of meat.

UK:

It is a madness. How shall the stars profit us? Will they lead us to a bear's den, or where the deer foregather, or break for us great bones that we come at their marrow? Will they tell us anything at all? Wait thou until the night, and we shall peer forth from between the boulders, and all men shall take note that the stars cannot whisper... Yet it may be that they are pieces of the day. This is a deep matter.

OAN:

Ay! they are pieces of the moon!

UK:

What further madness is this ? How shall they be pieces of two things that are not the same ? Also it was not thus in the song.

OAN:

I will make me a new song. We do change the shape of wood and stone, but a song is made out of nothing. Ho ! ho ! I can fashion things from nothing ! Also I say that the stars come down at morning and become the dew.

UK:

Let us have no more of these stars. It may be that a song is a good thing, if it be of what a man knoweth. Thus, if thou singest of my club, or of the bear that I slew, of the stain on the Stone, or the cave and the warm leaves in the cave, it might be well.

OAN:

I will make thee a song of Ala !

UK (*furiously*):

Thou shalt make me no such song ! Thou shalt make me a song of the deer-liver that thou hast eaten ! Did I not give to thee of the liver of the she-deer, because thou didst bring me crawfish ?

OAN:

Truly I did eat of the liver of the she-deer; but to sing thereof is another matter.

UK:

It was no labour for thee to sing of the stars. See now our clubs and casting-stones, with which we slay flesh to eat; also the caves in which we dwell, and the Stone whereon we make sacrifice; wilt thou sing no song of those ?

OAN:

It may be that I shall sing thee songs of them. But now, as I strive here to sing of the doe's liver, no words are born unto me: I can but sing, "O liver ! O red liver !"

UK:

That is a good song: thou seest that the liver is red. It is red as blood.

OAN:

But I love not the liver, save to eat of it.

UK:

Yet the song of it is good. When the moon is full we shall sing it about the Stone. We shall beat upon our breasts and sing, "O liver ! O red liver !" And all the women in the caves shall be affrightened.

OAN:

I will not have that song of the liver ! It shall be OK's song; the tribe must say, "Ok hath made the song !"

OK:

Ay ! I shall be a great singer; I shall sing of a wolf's heart, and say, "Behold, it is red !"

UK:

Thou art a fool, and shalt sing only, "Hai, hai !" as thy father before thee. But OAN shall make me a song of my club, for the women listen to his songs.

OAN:

I will make thee no songs, neither of thy club, nor thy cave, nor thy doe's-liver. Yea ! though thou give me no more flesh, yet will I live alone in the forest, and eat the seed of grasses, and likewise rabbits, that are easily snared. And I will sleep in a tree-top, and I will sing nightly:

> The bright day is gone.
> The night maketh me sad, sad, sad,
>   sad, sad, sad —

UK:

OK and UN, arise and slay !
(*OK and UN rush upon OAN, who stoops and picks up two casting-stones, with one of which he strikes OK between the eyes, and with the other mashes the hand of UN, so that he drops his club. UK arises.*)

UK:

Behold ! Gurr cometh ! he cometh swiftly from the wood !
(*The Tribe, including OAN and ALA, rush for the cave-mouths. As OAN passes UK, the latter runs behind OAN and crushes his skull with a blow of his club.*)

UK:

O men ! O men with the heart of hyenas ! Behold, Gurr cometh not ! I did but strive to deceive you, that I might the more easily slay this singer, who is very swift of foot. . . . Gather ye before me, for I would speak wisdom. . . It is not well that there be any song among us other than what our fathers sang in the past, or, if there be songs, let them be of such matters as are of common understanding. If a man sing of a deer, so shall he be drawn, it may be, to go forth and slay a deer, or even a moose. And if he sing of his casting-stones, it may be that he become more apt in the use thereof. And if he sing of his cave, it may be that he shall defend it more stoutly when Gurr teareth at the boulders. But it is a vain thing to make songs of the stars, that seem scornful even of me; or of the moon, which is never two nights the same; or of the day, which goeth about its business and will not linger though one pierce a she-babe with a flint. But as for me, I would have none of these songs. For if I sing of such in the council, how shall I keep my wits ? And if I think thereof, when at the chase, it may be that I babble it forth, and the meat hear and escape. And ere it be time to eat, I do give my mind solely to the care of my hunting-gear. And if one sing when eating, he may fall short of his just portion. And when one hath eaten, doth not he go straightway to sleep ? So where shall men find a space for singing ? But do ye as ye will: as for me, I will have none of these songs and stars.

Be it also known to all the women that if, remembering these wild words of **OAN**, they do sing them to themselves, or teach them to the young ones, they shall be beaten with brambles. Cause swiftly that the wife of **OK** cease from her wailing, and bring hither the horses that were slain yesterday, that I may apportion them. Had **OAN** wisdom, he might have eaten thereof; and had a mammoth fallen into our pit, he might have feasted many days. But **OAN** was a fool !

UN:

OAN was a fool !

ALL THE TRIBE:

OAN was a fool !

THE END

Jack and Charmian on the beach in Waikiki, 1915.

Charmian dressed for horse riding, with their dog, Possum.

Jack and Charmian photographed at a friends wedding reception.

SECTION G

BOOK INSCRIPTIONS

This section contains inscriptions made by Jack London on the inside cover of his first editions, which he sent to his second wife Charmian, first wife Bessie Maddern and their children: Joan and Becky London.

Inscriptions are included in this collection because many of them contain poetry or poetic verse, which illustrate and support the central theme of this book that Jack London was essentially a poet and greatly influence by poetry. Every opportunity to write, unrestrained by the need to satisfy his primary function as a fiction and nonfiction writer and thereby earn a living, he took and more often than not wrote poetry.

Many of the inscriptions here are of a very personal nature and display great affection and love for his family as might be expected of a passionate man.

The structure of this section is broken into two separate parts. First are those inscriptions addressed to Charmian (second wife) and are numbered chronologically according to the publication date. In a few instances Jack London wrote inscriptions in separate books but these appear under the original publication number and in date order of the inscription. Second are the inscriptions to Jack London's first wife and children. Again these are arranged and numbered in chronological order of publication. Each inscription is reproduced as written by Jack London.

BOOK INSCRIPTIONS

Charmian Kittredge-London

(The book numbers refer to published books in Appendix C)

1. **The Son of the Wolf**   Houghton Mifflin, 1900

    Dear Charmian—my first reviewer
    With best regards, Jack London

2. **The God of His Fathers**   McClure, Phillips and Co., 1901

    To Charmian:—

    "The bird of life is singing in the Sun,
    Short is his song, nor only just began—
    A call, a trill, a rapture, then—so soon
    A silence, and the song is done—is done."

    From Jack London   The Bungalow—June 26, 1903

    (NOTE: Quatrain (3rd) on page 36 from Rubáiyát of Omar Khayyám: A Paraphrase from Several Literal Translations (Pub. 1897) *by Omar Khayyam and Richard Le Gallienne (1866-1947).*

3. **Children of the Frost**   The Macmillan Co., 1902

    Dear Charmian—Greetings, Jack

4. **The Cruise of the Dazzler**   The Century Co., 1902

    Dear Charmian—

    In memory of the "Jessie E" and the run home before the wind.

    Jack London   The Bungalow   Feb. 25, 1903

4. **The Cruise of the Dazzler**   Hodder Stoughton, 1906

    Dear Mate,

And soon we sail on own cruise, "The Cruise of the Snark"—
and we shall be mates around the whole round world.
Your Mate

Wake Robin Lodge,   Oct. 9, 1906

5   *A Daughter of the Snows*   J. B. Lippincott, 1902

Dear Charmian—Happy New Year

1904 Jack.   February 1903

6   *The Kempton-Wace Letters*   (*First copy*) The Macmillan Co., 1903

To Charmian—

"Oh, my beloved, fill the cup that clears
To-day of past Regrets and future Fears:
To–morrow!—Why, To-morrow I may be
Myself with Yesterday's Seven thousand years."

Jack   The Bungalow, June 6, 1903

(*NOTE: Quatrain XXI from* The Rubaiyat, *by Omar Khayyám*)

6   *The Kempton-Wace Letters*   (*First copy—second inscription*)

To my wife—

One hour of love is worth a century of science.

Mate.   Feb. 28, 1906.

6   *The Kempton-Wace Letters*   (*Second copy*)

Charmian—Here's hopin' Jack Dec. 31, 1903

6   *The Kempton-Wace Letters*   (*Second copy—second inscription*)

John Ball to Charmian Kittredge
through the hand of Anna Strunsky

"What else shall ye lack when ye lack masters? We shall not
lack for the fields ye have tilled, nor the houses ye have built,

nor the cloth ye have woven; all these shall be yours, and whatso ye will of all that the earth beareth; then shall no man mow the deep grass for another, while his own kine lack cow meat; and he that soweth shall reap, and the reaper shall eat in fellowship the harvest that in fellowship he hath won; and he that buildeth a house shall live in it with those that he listeth of his free will."

(Note: This extract of text—a quote from the character John Ball—is from The Dream of John Ball *by William Morris, which was first serialized in* The Commonweal *(Nov 13, 1886–Jan 22, 1887). It also appears on page 53, of the Longmans' Pocket Library edition 1913,* The Dream of John Ball and A King's Lesson.*)*

7   **The Call of the Wild**   The Macmillan Co., 1903

To Charmian—

"A book of verse underneath the bough,
A jug of wine, a Loaf of Bread—and Thou
Besides me singing in the Wilderness—
Oh, Wilderness were Paradise enow!"

From Jack London,   July 21, 1903

(*NOTE: Quatrain XII from* The Rubaiyat, *by Omar Khayyám*)

7   **The Call of the Wild** (*second copy*)

To Charmian—

"So, glady, from the songs of modern speech
Men turn, and see the stars & feel the free
Shrill wind beyond the close of heavy flowers,
And, through the music of the languid hours,
They hear the ocean on a western beach,
The surge and the thunder of the Odyssey."

From Jack London.   July 22, 1903

(*NOTE: Taken from a poem called "Odyssey" by Andrew Laing*)

7   **The Call of the Wild** (third copy)   The Macmillan Co., 1912 (Edition)

This night the Wolf House, our dream house, went up in smoke
My Woman:—

It was many dear years ago when I first gave you a copy of this book—in the days when I was hearing love call. And never has that same love called more loudly than it calls now in this year 1913, when my arms are still full of you and my heart still full of you.

    Jack London   Glen Ellen, California, Aug. 22, 1913

8   The People of the Abyss   The Macmillan Co., 1903

    Dear Charmian

    Jack   December 31, 1903

And you are still Dear Charmian, and in addition, dearer Charmian, and dearest Charmian. I am still Jack, & you & I are "Mates".

    Jack London,   Glen Ellen, California, November 23, 1906

9   The Faith of Men   The Macmillan Co., 1904

    Dear Charmian: –
    You know, I know, and what the deuce do we care who else knows?

    Jack.   Oakland, California   July 22, 1904

10 The Sea-Wolf   The Macmillan Co., 1904

    Dear Charmian –

    How can I give to you what you have so much helped to make?

    Jack.   Oakland, California November 27, 1904

11 War of the Classes   The Macmillan Co., 1905

Dear Mate —

Just to tell you that you are more mate than ever, and that the years to come are bound to see us very happy.

 Mate.   Glen Ellen,   April 28, 1905

12 *The Game*   The Macmillan Co., 1905

Dear Mate –

Whose voice and touch are quick to soothe, and who, with a firm hand, has helped me to emerge from my "long sickness" so that I might look upon the world again clear-eyed.

 From your Mate.   Glen Ellen,   July 17/05

13 *Tales of the Fish Patrol*   The Macmillan Co., 1905

Dear Mate –

The time grows short .... Love's waiting time. The days grow short. The frost is in the air. The Red Gods call to us. We hurl ourselves across the world—to meet again and not to part.

Your own Mate   Jack London.
Wake Robin Lodge, Glen Ellen, California   October 11, 1905

14 *Moon-Face*   The Macmillan Co., 1906

My Own Dear Mate

"There's a whisper down the field
Where the year has shot her yield
And the ricks stand gray in the sun,
Saying: Over, then come over,
For the bee has quit the clover,
—Our Sonoma Summer's done.

You have heard the beat of the off-shore wind
And the thresh of the deep-sea rain;
You have heard the song, how long, how long?
Pull out on the trail again!"

From her Mate
Jack London   Glen Ellen, California Sept. 22, 1906

(*NOTE: This is the first stanza of a poem called "L'Envoi" from the book,* From Barrack-Room Ballads, *by Rudyard Kipling.*)

15 *White Fang*   The Macmillan Co., 1906

Dearest Mate:

I love you, Mate

Glen Ellen, Calif.,   Oct. 11, 1906

Our Book (*At bottom of page*)

16 *Scorn of Women*   The Macmillan Co., 1906

To the Dear Little Woman:

Who has toiled sore with me over these pages and yet found time to make me very, very happy.
With a love to-day that makes our early love a puny thing.

Your Mate and Husband,
Jack London   Wake Robin Lodge   Nov. 29, 1906

17 *Before Adam*   The Macmillan Co., 1907

My own Dear Mate-Woman: –

I have read Schopenhauer, and Weininger, and all the German misogynists, and still I love you. Such is my chemism—our chemism, rather.

Your Mate-Man
Jack London!   Oakland, Calif.,   March 12, 1907

18 *Love of Life*   The Macmillan Co., 1907

Dear Mate-Woman:—

There is within these pages a story you wot of well, wherein long ago I told of my love for you, and, more and better, of all you and your love meant and mean, to me.

Jack London   Wake Robin Lodge   Nov. 23, 1909

19 The Road   The Macmillan Co., 1907

(Note: *On a fly-sheet before the dedication he wrote out four stanzas (not in the original order) from his own poem "The Worker and the Tramp" but with the last two verses of the last stanza reversed.*)

Heaven bless you, my friend—
You, the man who won't sweat;
Here's a quarter to spend.

Your course I commend,
nor regard with regret;
Heaven bless you, my friend.

On you I depend
For my works, don't forget,
Here's a quarter to spend.

Ah! you comprehend
That I owe you a debt;
Here's a quarter to spend;
Heaven bless you my friend.

Jack London
P.S. - Written many years ago.   Oct. 9, 1910.

(*After the poem, on the reverse of a separate page, he wrote the following.*)

Dearest My Woman: –

Whose efficient hands I love—the hands that have worked for me for long hours and many, swiftly and deftly, and beautifully in the making of music; the hands that have steered the <u>Snark</u> through wild passages and rough seas, that do not tremble on a trigger, that are sure and strong on the reins of a thoroughbred or an untamed Marquesan stallion; the hands that are sweet with love as they pass through my hair, firm with comradeship as they grip mine, and that soothe as only they of all hands in the world can soothe.

Your Man and Lover
Jack London   Glen Ellen,   Oct. 10, 1910

20 *The Iron Heel*   The Macmillan Co., 1908

Dearest Heart:—

"We that have been what we've been.... We that have seen what we've seen"—we may not see these particular things come to pass, but certain it is that we shall see big things of some sort come to pass.

Mate-Man   Wake Robin   May 2, 1910

21 *Martin Eden*   The Macmillan Co., 1909

Dearest Mate-Woman: —

You see, Martin Eden did not have you.

Mate-Man   Wake Robin Lodge   Oct. 3, 1909
(Opposite the copyright page)

Let me live my years in the heat of blood!
Let me lie drunken with the dreamer's wine!
Let me not see this soul-house built of mud
Go toppling to the dust, a vacant shrine!

(NOTE: This is the first stanza of a poem called "Let me live my years" from the book, Quest by John Gueisenau Neihardt.)

22 *Lost Face*   The Macmillan Co., 1910

Dearest Heart —

See, here, the first wee bit of young pulsating life that knit our hearts warmly; yet now, to-day, we are expectant of another young pulsating bit that has already more warmly knit our hearts together than anything else we have ever experienced.

Your own Mate-Man.   Wake Robin   May 10, 1910

23 **Revolution and Other Essays**　　　　The Macmillan Co., 1910

   My Mate-Woman—

   Not that I shall be able to tell you anything about revolution—you who in a few short weeks from now, will be prime mover in turning our Wake Robin household upside down with the most delicious and lovable revolution that we can ever hope to experience.

   　Mate-Man　　　　Wake Robin Lodge　　April 24, 1910

24 **Burning Daylight**　　　　　　　The Macmillan Co., 1910

   A Sweet land, Mate-Woman, an almighty sweet land you and I have chosen—our Valley of the Moon.

   　Your Own Man
   　Jack London　　　　Wake Robin,　　Oct. 15, 1910.

25 **Theft**　　　　　　　　　　　　The Macmillan Co., 1910

   Dear My-Woman:—

   How our days continue to grow fuller and sweeter!
   Your Lover-Man,
   Jack London　　　Glen Ellen,　　December 2, 1910

26 **When God Laughs**　　　　　　The Macmillan Co., 1911

   My Own Dear Woman:—

   The years come, and the years go, our friends come and go, some few of them stick—and you and I stick better than any or all.

   　Jack London　　　Wake Robin Lodge,　　Feb. 16, 1911

27 **Adventure**　　　　　　　　　　The Macmillan Co., 1911

   Dearest Mate Woman: –

   Scenes here, dear to you and me, shared together by us, in the days when we still sailed the "Snark" on her far-wandering through the cannibal isles.

Your Lover-Husband,
Jack London   Glen Ellen,   Mar. 19, 1911

28 *The Cruise of the Snark*   The Macmillan Co., 1911

To Charmian: –

The mate of the <u>Snark</u>, who took the wheel, night or day, when entering or leaving port, or running a passage, who took the wheel in every emergency, and who wept, after two years of sailing, when the voyage was discontinued.

Jack London   The Ranch   Sept. 12, 1911

29 *South Sea Tales*   The Macmillan Co., 1911

Dearest Mate-Woman: –

And can we say, after all these years, that we have ever been happier than we are happy right now?

Your Mate-Man
The Ranch   Glen Ellen, Calif.,   Oct. 14, 1911

30 *The House of Pride*   The Macmillan Co., 1912

Mate Woman: –

These, too, are our isles, and seas, and peoples, and we have lived with them, you and I, in the tales they have lived.

Wolf Man   Glen Ellen, Calif.,   Aug. 24, 1912

31 *A Son of the Sun*   Doubleday, Page & Co., 1912

Dear White Woman: –

We have sailed these turquoise seas together; together lifted these palm-fronded isles out of the sea's depths; and together known these perishing sons of the sun. We know! We know!

Your Wolf Man   Glen Ellen, Aug. 24, 1912

32 *Smoke Bellew*   The Century Co., 1912

Dearest Mate-Woman: –
I am stilled filled with joy of your voice that was mine last night when you sang, Sometimes, more than clearly wronglet concept of you, there are fiber-sounds in your throat that tell me all the lovableness of you, and that I love as madly as I have always madly loved all the rest of you.

Wolf-Man   Oct. 2, 1912

33 *The Night Born*   The Century Co., 1913

Dear My-Woman: –

The seasons come and go, the years slide together in the long backward trail, and yet you and I remain, welded with our arms about each other, moving onward together and unafraid of any future.

Your man,
Jack London   The Ranch,   Mar. 13, 1913

34 *The Abysmal Brute*   The Century Co., 1913

Dear My-Woman:—

The years pass, we live much, and yet, to me, I find but one vindication for living, but one bribe for living—and the vindication is you, the bribe is you.

Your Lover,
Jack London   Glen Ellen ,   May 27, 1913

35 *John Barleycorn*   The Century Co., 1913

Dear Mate-Woman:—

You know you have helped me bury the Long Sickness and the White Logic.

Your Mate-man
Jack London   The Ranch,   Aug. 22, 1913

36 *The Valley of the Moon* The Macmillan Co., 1913

Dear My-Woman –

This is our "Book of Love," here in our "Valley of the Moon," where we have lived & known our love ever since that day you rode with me to the divide of the Napa Hills—ay, and before that, before that.

Jack London   The Ranch, Glen Ellen   March 7, 1914

37 *The Strength of the Strong* The Macmillan Co., 1914

Dear My Mate-Woman: -

Back again from Vera Cruz and all the world, you back with me from the war-game, I am almost driven to assert that our little war-game adventure was as sweet & fine as our first honeymoon.

Your mate
Jack London   June 26, 1914

38 *The Mutiny of the Elsinore* The Macmillan Co., 1914

Dear Mate-Woman –

We, too, have made this voyage together, &, in all happiness, known the winter north Atlantic, the pamperos of the Plate, and the Sou'west gales & Great West Wind Drift of the Horn. And we "made westing," as we have made westing in all the years since we first loved.

Mate-Man   Sept. 21, 1914
9 yrs. married (*In the margin*)

39 *The Scarlet Plague* The Macmillan Co., 1915

My Mate-Woman:—

And here, in blessed Hawaii, eight years after our voyage here in our own speck boat, we find ourselves, not mere again, but more bound to each other than then & than ever.

Mate Man
Jack London   Honolulu, Hawaii   July 16, 1915

40 *The Star Rover*   The Macmillan Co., 1915

Dearest Wife-Woman:—

Will we ever forget the "Roamer" days and nights when these pages were being written and when we sailed, and sailed, and funned & funned and loved & loved, dear heart?

Mate & Husband Man   Oct. 19,1915.

(*Note: This book was first published under the title* The Jacket *by Mills and Boon Ltd, London in July 1915 and the US edition was published in October 1915.*)

41 *The Acorn Planter*   The Macmillan Co., 1916

Darlingest:—

You remember when I wrote this, you typed it, and <u>we</u> joy-sailed together on the good, old, dear, & forever dear "Roamer"?
Everest,
alias
Husband-Mate
alias
Jack London   Aug. 6/16

42 *The Little Lady of the Big House*   The Macmillan Co., 1916

Dearest Mate:—

The years pass. You and I pass. But yet our love abides—more firmly, more deeply, more surely, for we have built our love for each other, not upon the sand, but upon the rock.

Your Lover-Husband
Jack London   August 6, 1916

43 *The Turtles of Tasman*   The Macmillan Co., 1916

Dearest Mate:

After it all, and it all, and it all, here we are, all in all, all in all.

Sometimes I just want to get up on top of Sonoma Mountain and shout to the world about you and me.
Arms ever around and around.

Mate-Man   The Ranch   Oct. 6, 1916

44 *The Turtles of Tasman*   The Macmillan Co., 1917

Darlingest

I love you

Your Uxorist

(Note: Inscription written on 3 strips of paper that were cut out and pasted into the book)

Bess Madden London, the mother of Bess and Joan.

Jack London with daughters Bess [left] and Joan [right].

BOOK INSCRIPTIONS

Bessie Maddern, Joan London and Becky London

1 ***The Son of the Wolf***   Houghton-Mifflin & Co, 1900

Dear Mother-Girl—

From

Daddy-Boy   Oakland, Calif., July 27, 1904

2 ***The God of His Fathers***   McClure, Phillips and Co., 1901

Dear Mother-Girl

Here's an English edition in return for the American edition I borrowed from you.

With love from
Daddy-Boy   Oakland, Calif., Nov., 1904

(Obviously this inscription appears on the English edition which came out in 1904. It is placed here in the order of the American first edition.)

3 ***Children of the Frost***   The Macmillan Co. Co., 1902

Dearest Bess,

"The first book of mine, all for your own," you said. But what matters it? Am I not all your own, your

Daddy-Boy?   The Bungalow   Christmas, 1902

4 ***The Cruise of the Dazzler***   The Century Co., 1902

Dear Mother-Girl—

Some day you can read this aloud to the two youngsters.

With love from
Daddy-Boy.   Piedmont, California, October, 1902.

Section G - Book Inscriptions

5 *A Daughter of the Snows*   J. B. Lippincott Co. 1902

Dear Mother-Girl—

With love from

Daddy-Boy   Piedmont, Calif., Christmas 1902.

7 *The Call of the Wild*   The Macmillan Co., 1903

Dear, dear Mother-Girl—

Daddy-Boy   July 22, 1903

8 *The People of the Abyss*   The Macmillan Co., 1903

Dear Mother-Girl—

Know that such you will always be to me—

Daddy-Boy.   Oakland, Calif., November 12, 1903

9 *The Faith of Men*   The Macmillan Co., 1904

Dear Mother-Girl—

I can only repeat, as you will always be to me—

Daddy-Boy   July 8, 1904

10 *The Sea-Wolf*   The Macmillan Co., 1904

Dear Mother-Girl—

With best love from

Daddy-Boy.   Oakland, Calif., Nov. 21, 1904

11 *War of the Classes*   The Macmillan Co., 1905

Dear Mother-Girl—

With Love from
Daddy-Boy   Oakland, May 21, 1905.

*12 **The Game***　　　　　　　　　　　The Macmillan Co., 1905

Dear Mother-Girl—

With love, from

Daddy-Boy　　　　　　Oakland, July 9, 1905

*13 **Tales of the Fish Patrol***　　　　　　The Macmillan Co., 1905

Dear Mother-Girl—

Find here, sometimes hinted, sometimes told, and some-times made different, the days of my boyhood when I, too, was on the Fish Patrol—

With love from
Daddy-Boy　　　　　　Glen Ellen, Calif., March 2, 1906

*14 **Moon-Face***　　　　　　　　　　The Macmillan Co., 1906

Dear Mother-Girl—

Not much herein—just another book.

With love,
Daddy-Boy.　　　　　　Glen Ellen, Calif., Oct., 3, 1906

*15 **White Fang***　　　　　　　　　　The Macmillan Co., 1906

Dear Mother-Girl—

Greeting and best wishes from

Daddy-Boy　　　　　　Glen Ellen, Calif., Oct., 30, 1906

*16 **Scorn of Women***　　　　　　　　The Macmillan Co., 1906

Dear Mother-Girl—

My first play; not a very fortunate venture; but I'll do better Next time. Be charitable when you read it.

With love from,
Daddy-Boy.　　　　　　Oakland, Calif., December 3, 1906

21 *Martin Eden*   The Macmillan Co., 1909

Dear Bessie—

Now do you remember ever seeing "Higginbotham's Cash Store?"

Affectionately yours,
Jack London   Glen Ellen, March 23, 1910.

22 *Lost Face*   The Macmillan Co., 1910

Dear Bessie—

My latest. Do tell me how you like it "The wit of Porportuk," & the others, too.

Jack London   Glen Ellen, Calif., March 23/1910.

23 *Revolution and Other Essays*   The Macmillan Co., 1910

Dear Bessie—

"Oh God, make no more giants:
Elevate the race."

With love from,
Jack London   Glen Ellen, Calif., May 11, 1910.

24 *Burning Daylight*   The Macmillan Co., 1910

Dear Bessie—

Just one more of the many I shall write ere I cease and be dust.

Affectionately,
Jack London   Glen Ellen, November 15, 1910.

25 *Theft*   The Macmillan Co., 1910

Dear Bessie—

Here's another for the shelf. It looks as if I'm trying to see how many books I can publish before I die.

Jack London   Glen Ellen, Dec. 2, 1910

26 *When God Laughs*   The Macmillan Co., 1911

Dear Bessie:—

God often laughs—especially at glass windows.

Jack London   Glen Ellen, Calif., Feb. 16, 1911.

27 *Adventure*   The Macmillan Co., 1911

Dear Bessie:—

Some of the scenes through which we sailed the "Snark."

Jack London   Glen Ellen, Calif., March 19, 1911.

28 *The Cruise of the Snark*   The Macmillan Co., 1911

Just a few highlights, here & there, on our cruise. We loved it, more and more as the days went by, and we sorrowed to give it up.

Jack London   Glen Ellen, Calif., Sept. 12, 1911.

29 *South Sea Tales*   The Macmillan Co., 1911

Dear Bessie:—

Just phases of life, that is as different in the South Seas as It is on all other parts of the earth's surface.

Jack London   Glen Ellen, Oct. 20, 1911.

30 *The House of Pride*   The Macmillan Co., 1912

Dear Bessie:—

Affectionately thine,

Jack London   Glen Ellen, Calif., Aug. 24, 1912.

30 The House of Pride (*Second copy*)

Dear Joan,

I am just now writing a new series of Hawaiian stories which I think you'll like better than the ones herein.

Daddy,   Honolulu, T.H. July 17, 1916

31 A Son of the Sun   Doubleday, Page & Co., 1912

Dear Bessie:—

"And write before I die:
'E liked it all!'"

Jack London   Glen Ellen, Calif., Aug. 24, 1912.

32 Smoke Bellew   The Century Co., 1912

Dear Bessie:—

More Klondike yarns. I've written a hundred of them. Well, What do you think?

Affectionately Yours,
Jack London   Glen Ellen, Oct. 2, 1912.

34 The Abysmal Brute   The Century Co., 1913

Dear Bessie:—

Just a fight game yarn, and yet there's a lot of truth in it.

Affectionately yours,
Jack London   Glen Ellen, Calif., May 27, 1913

35 *John Barleycorn*   The Century Co., 1913

Dear Bessie:—

The first one of the ancient that arrives to go on the shelf in the Piedmont home.

Jack London   Glen Ellen, Calif., Aug. 22, 1913.

37 *The Strength of the Strong*   The Macmillan Co., 1914

Dear Joan—

Daddy   Aug. 6, 1916.

38 *Mutiny of the Elsinore*   The Macmillan Co., 1914

Dear Joan—

Daddy   August 6/16

41 *The Acorn Planter*   The Macmillan Co., 1916

Dear Joan:

Love

Daddy   Aug. 6, 1916.

43 *The Turtles of Tasman*   The Macmillan Co., 1916

Dear Joan & Bess:—

Yarns, just yarns. There may be some little meat of meaning in them. Who knows? Who knows?

Daddy   Oct. 7, 1916.

Appendix A

Jack London:

No 1
Magazine Sales
(From 1898 to 1900)

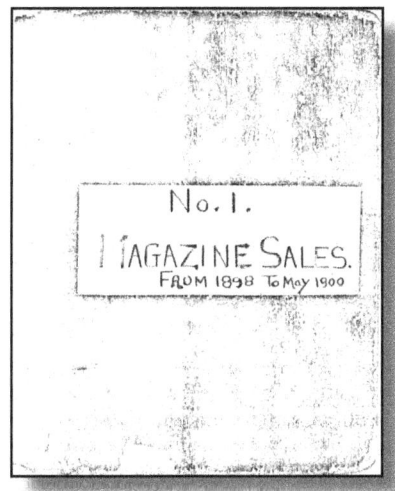

Above is the front cover and title page of Jack London's log-book called "No 1 Magazine Sales—from 1898 to May 1900." This cover is one of four log-books in total held at The Huntington Library, San Marino, CA. Presented here are 28 of the first 30 pages (25 & 26 omitted with no prosodic notes) of an 80 page log-book and in them is a wealth of information relating to London's prosodic studies and research into classical measures and verse construction, as well as many names and addresses. In later pages of this and the other three log-books there are countless details containing addresses, manuscript submissions, word counts, postage, dates and monies pay for publication.

However, London clearly used this first log-book as a poetry work book as well as a notebook. These 28 pages containing notes, detailed definitions and explanations of various types of poems, analysis (scansion) with examples of most of the measures of classical verse construction plus detailed studies of individual poems and their meters. With a few exceptions they were all transcribed from Robert F. Brewer's seminal book *Orthometry: A treatise on the Art of Versification and the Technicalities of Poetry*, (1893), first edition. Beneath each double page, where applicable, the citation will refer to the page where the information was taken in "*Orthometry* by Brewer."

Here for the first time, without doubt, the precise book from which Jack London self-taught himself the art of writing poetry is identified. It unequivocally establishes beyond any shadow of doubt that Jack London studied, in great detail and immense depth, the mechanics of writing poetry. He did not casually begin to write poetry but rather, consistent with eschewing formal education, methodically and with great care set about studying the art of versification, or in other words, how to write poetry correctly with classical measures.

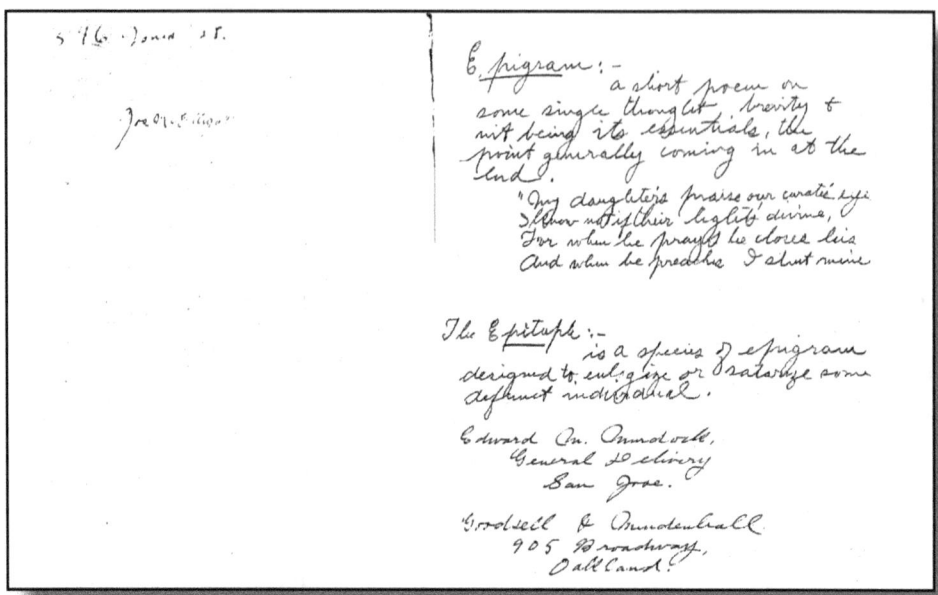

Pages 1 & 2: On page 2 (right), there are paraphrased notes on an "Epigram" and "Epitaph," with an epigram example quatrain below, taken from page 15 of *Orthometry* by Brewer. The quatrain, which is unattributed in the Brewer's book, is in fact an epigram by the Scottish Minister **George Outram**, called "On hearing a lady praise a Rev. Doctor's eye's" from *Lyrics, Legal and Miscellaneous* (Pub: Henry Glassford Bell–1874). The version that is used by Brewer is a later version because the words "...curate eye's" in the first verse, have been substituted from the original "...Doctor's eye's."

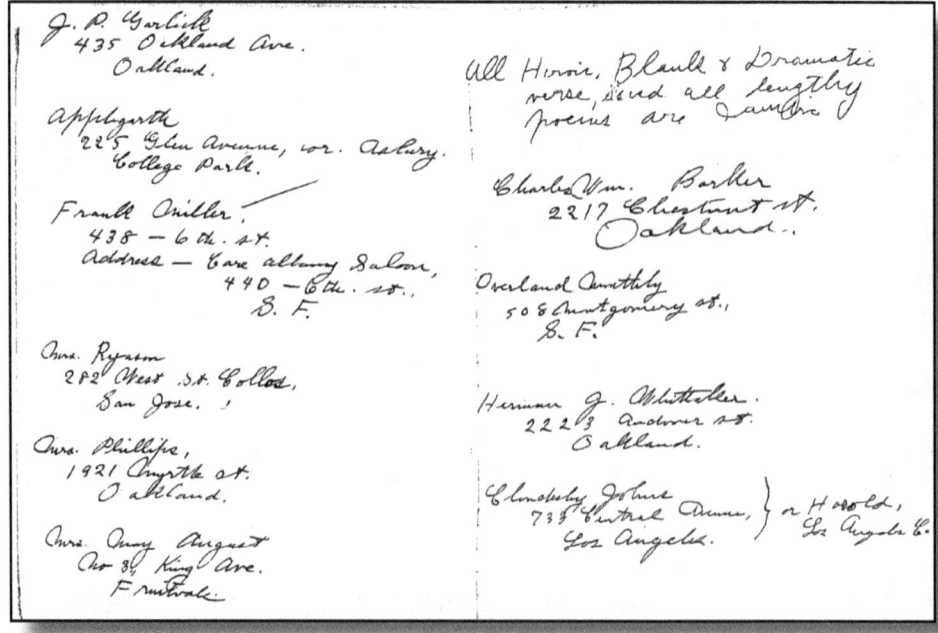

Pages 3 & 4: At the top of page 4 (right) is a sentence, which paraphrases a sentence appearing at the bottom of page 30 and top of page 31 of *Orthometry* by Brewer.

Appendix A: No 1–Magazine Sales

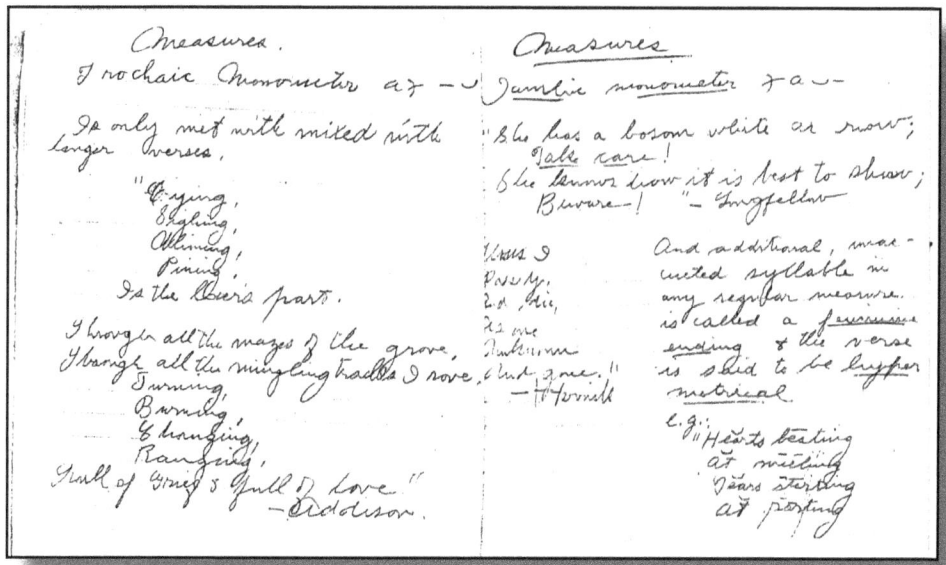

Pages 5 & 6: Page 5 (left): paraphrased notes on "Trochaic Monometer" and example by **Addison** are taken from page 40. Page 6 (right): title "Iambic monometer" with examples by **Longfellow** and **Herrick** taken from page 30; paraphrased note on "feminine ending," said to be "hypermetrical," with an unattributed example taken from page 32 of *Orthometry* by Brewer.

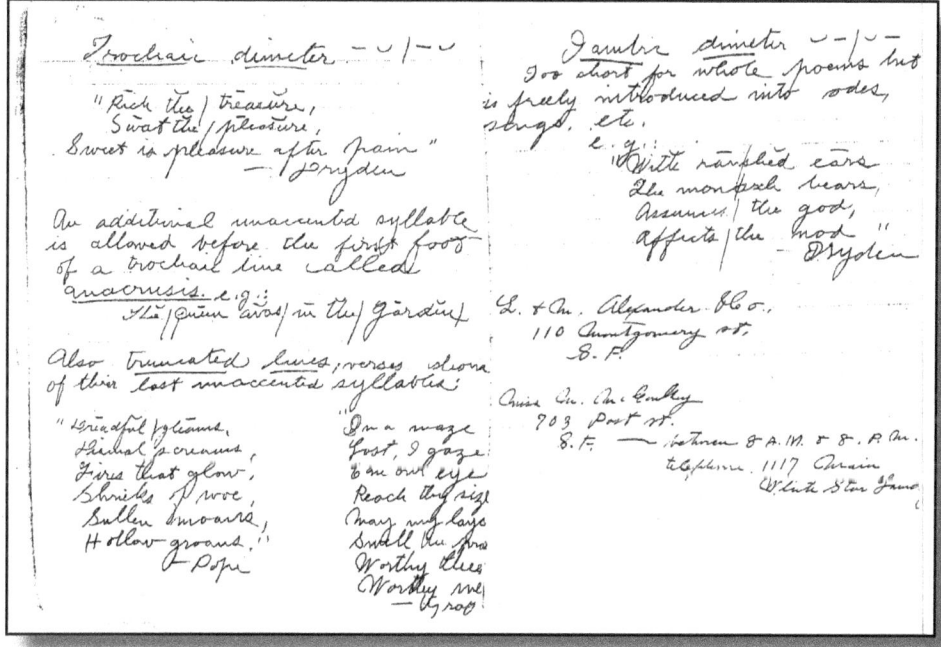

Pages 7 & 8: On Page 7 (left): title "Trochaic Dimeter" with the example by **Dryden** taken from page 40; paraphrased note about "anacrusis" with unattributed example and note about "truncated verses" with example by **Pope** taken from page 41; example by **Gray** (this is also by **Pope**, but erroneously attributed to **Gray** by Brewer) extends from page 41 to the top of page 42 from *Orthometry* by Brewer. On page 8 (right): the paraphrased note about "Iambic Dimeter" and the quatrain example by **Dryden** taken from page 32 of *Orthometry* by Brewer.

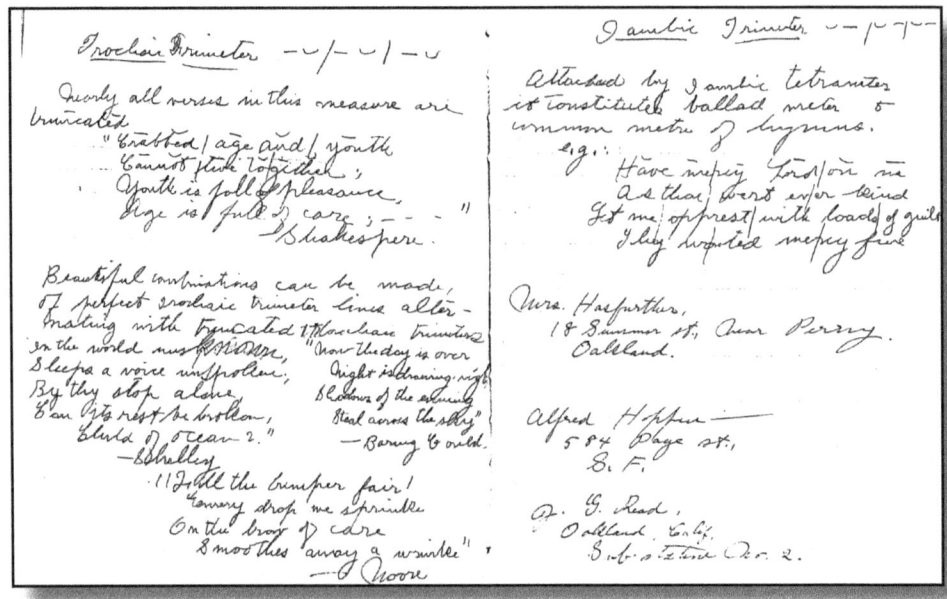

Pages 9 & 10: On page 9 (left): the title "Trochaic Trimeter," paraphrased notes on truncated versions and example by "**Shakespere**" (sic) are taken from page 42; paraphrased notes on alternating perfect, with truncated verses and examples by **Shelley**, **Baring Gould**, and **Moore**, are taken from page 43 of *Orthometry*. On page 10 (right): the title "Iambic Trimeter" with notes and example quatrain by **Dryden** (London failed to attribute the quatrain) are taken from page 33 of *Orthometry* by Brewer.

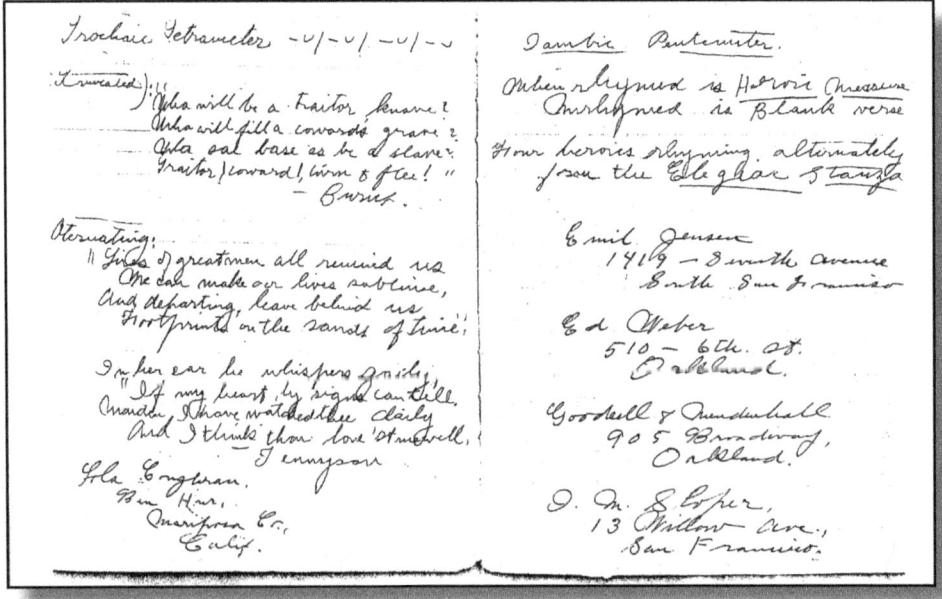

Pages 11 & 12: On page 11 (left): the title "Trochaic Tetrameter" is taken from page 43; the "truncated" example quatrain by **Burns** is taken from page 44; the "Alternating" example, with two quatrains by **Tennyson**, are taken from pages 44 and 45 of *Orthometry*. On page 12 (right): the title "Iambic Pentameter" and condensed paraphrased notes are taken from page 36 and 37 of *Orthometry* by Brewer.

Appendix A: No 1–Magazine Sales

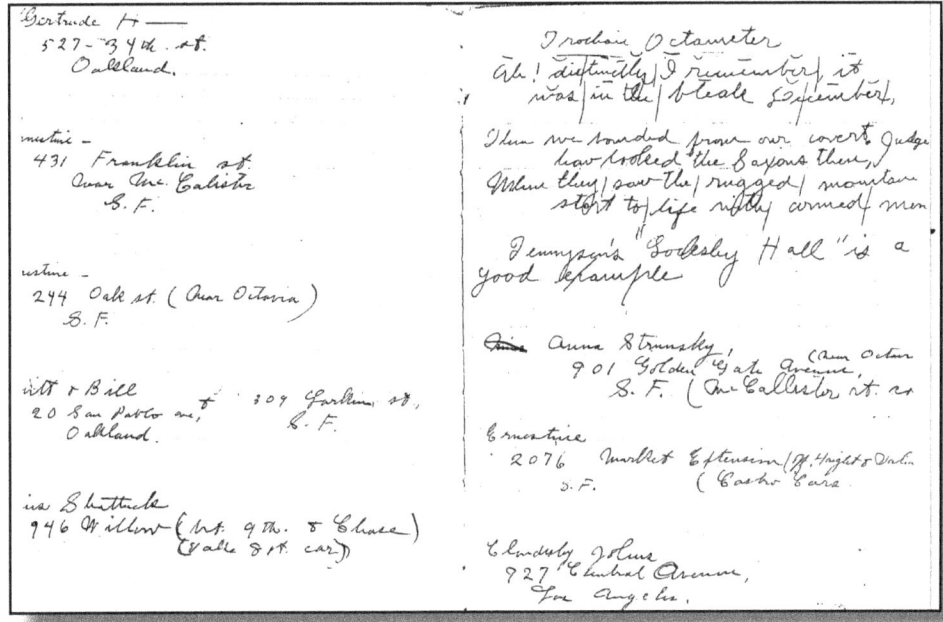

Pages 13 & 14: On page 14 (right): the title "Trochaic Octameter" taken from page 46; the top two verses by **Poe** are taken from the top of page 47; the next quatrain is by **Aytoun**, taken from page 47; note about **Tennyson's** "Locksley Hall" taken from page 46 of *Orthometry* by Brewer. Interesting to note the first address below this is that of **Anna Strunsky**, who was later to co-write, with Jack London, the book *The Kempton-Wace Letters* (1903).

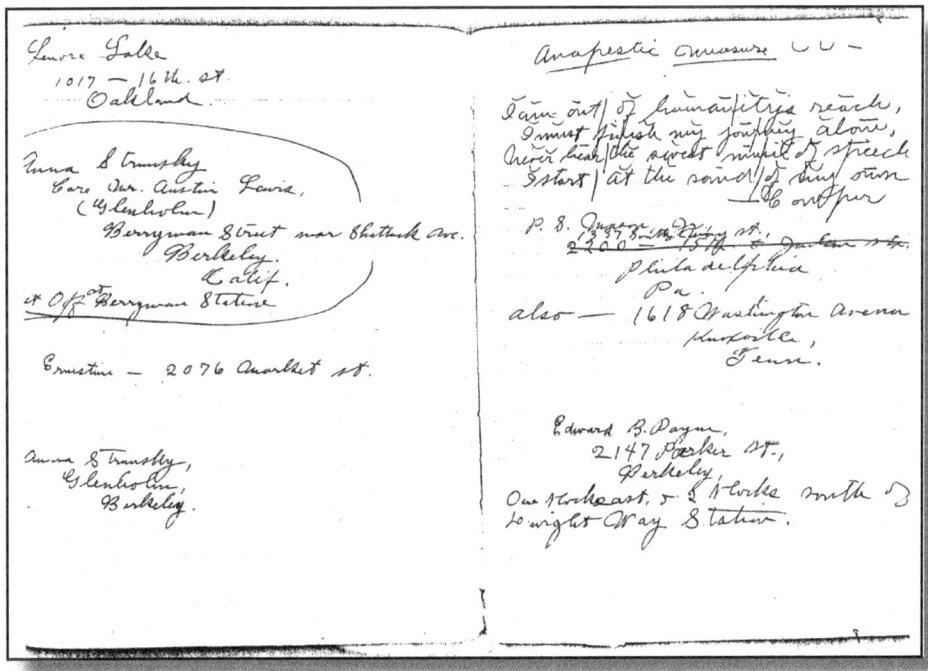

Page 15 & 16: On page 16 (right): the title "Anapestic Measure" is taken from page 47; the example quatrain is by **Cowper** and taken from page 48 of *Orthometry* by Brewer.

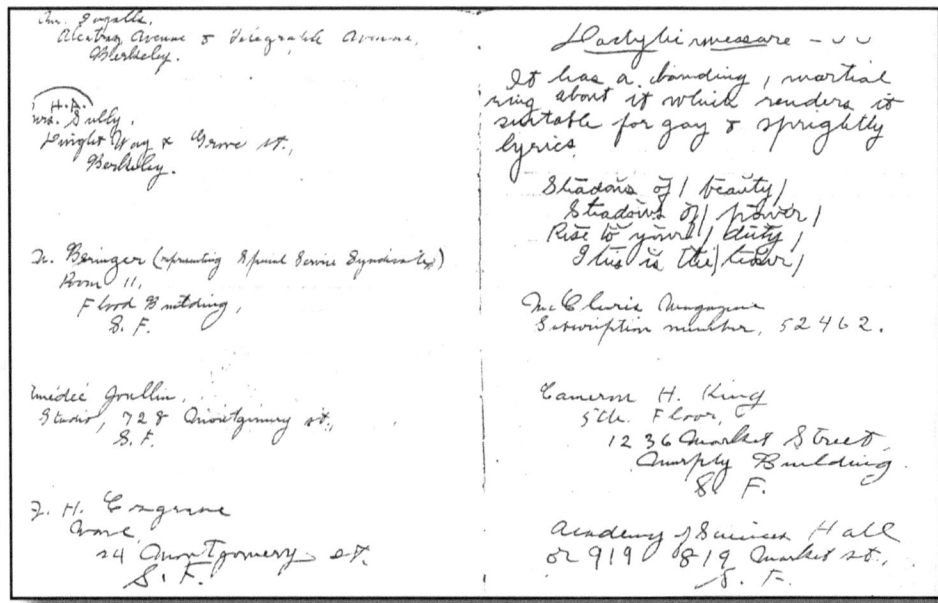

Page 17 & 18: On page 18 (right), the title "Dactylic measure," note and example quatrain by **Byron** (London failed to attribute) were taken from page 51 of *Othrometry* by Brewer.

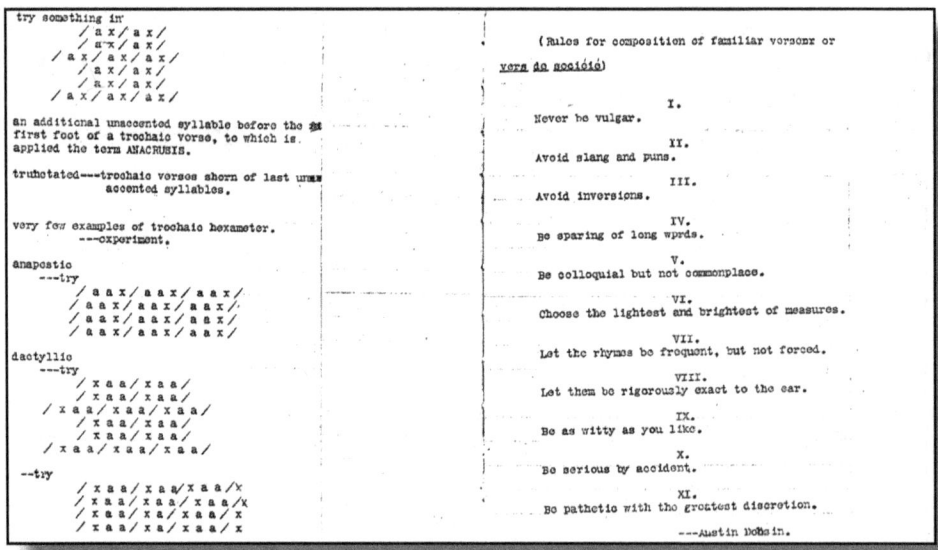

Pages 19 & 20: On page 19 (left): the first scansion (graphically represented by: a=long syllable, x=short syllable and /=foot division) is the example poem in mixed "trochaic dimeter" and "trimeter" by **Dryden** from page 40 and 41; the following note describing "anacrusis" is taken from page 41. The other notes and scansion of "anapestic" and "dactylic" (sic) meters are taken from pages 47 and 51 of *Orthometry*. On page 20 (right), London has copied a set of "Rules for composing familiar verse or vers de société," attributed to **Austin Dobsin** (London meant **Henry Austin Dobson** (1840-1921)–English poet). This poetic genre is particularly apt for London because he did write light verse. In fact there was a 12th (XII) rule: "Never ask if the writer of these rules has observed them himself." Apparently **Dobson** wrote them at the request of Brander Matthews (American Book Reviewer) in about 1890. London most probably read and copied them from a literary review written by Matthews.

Appendix A: No 1–Magazine Sales

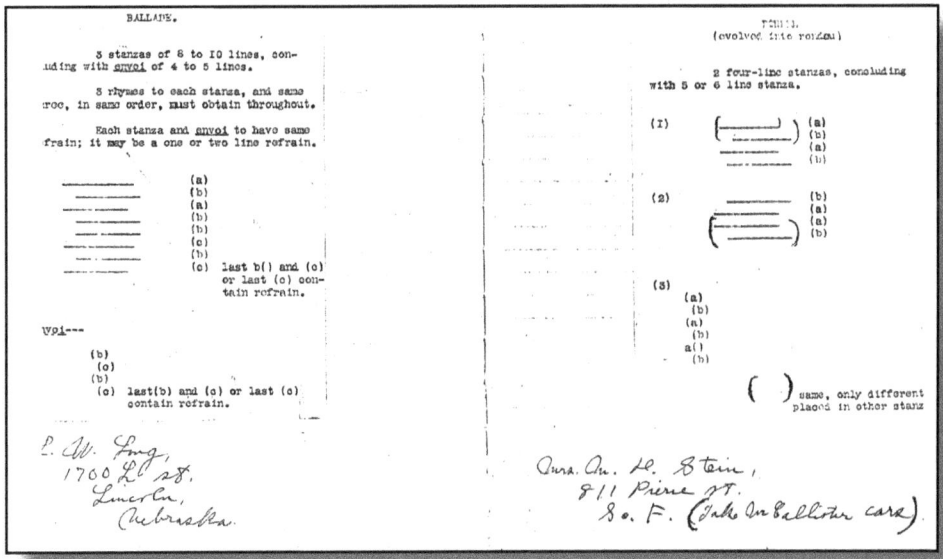

Page 21 & 22: On page 21 (left), London paraphrases the description of a "Ballade" and "envoi" with a schematic representation of the rhyming pattern of the stanza and envoi of a poem by **Clifford Scollard**, taken from pages 240 and 241. On page 22 (right), a brief paraphrased note about "Rondel" is taken from page 243, with a schematic representation of the rhyming pattern for an example poem by **John Cameron Grant**, taken from page 244 of *Orthometry* by Brewer.

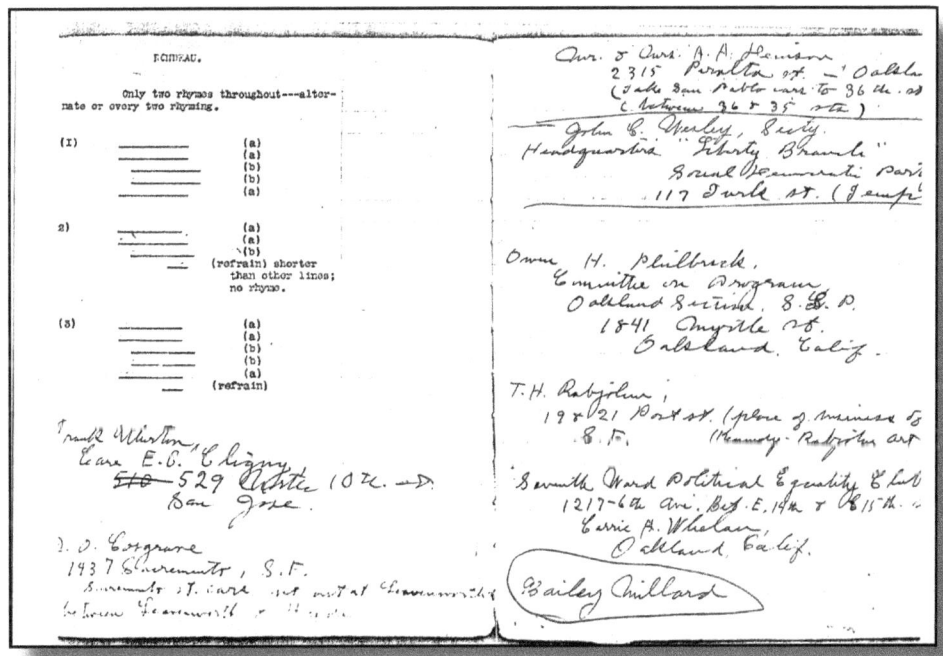

Page 23 & 24: On page 23 (left), London briefly paraphrases the description of the "Rondeau" taken from page 245, with a schematic representation of the rhyming pattern for an example poem by **Charles G.D. Roberts**, taken from the bottom of page 245 and the top of page 246 of *Orthometry* by Brewer.

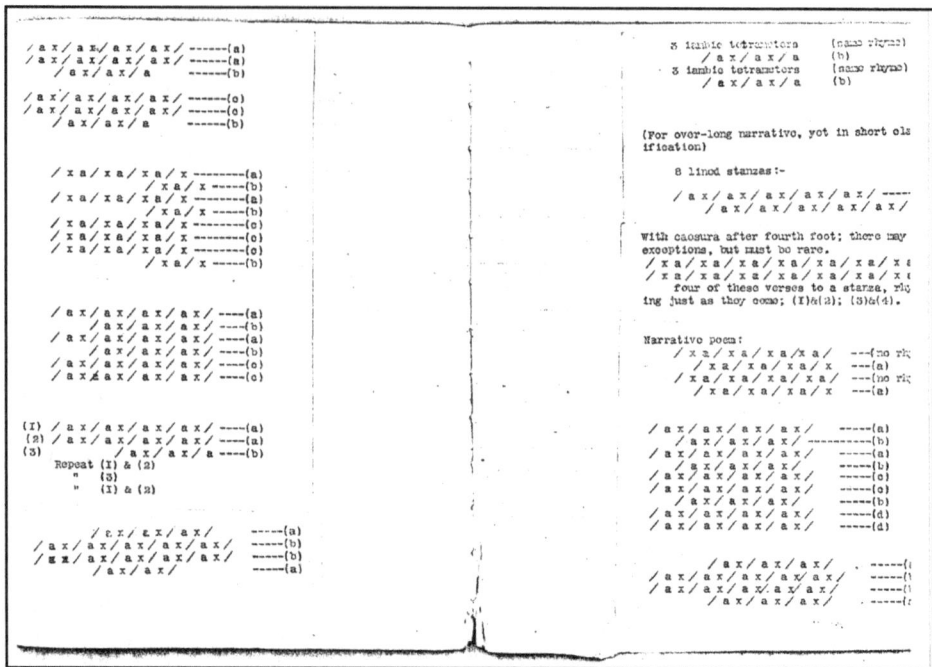

Page 27 & 28: On page 27 (left), there are scansions of a variety of meters both iambic and trochee with truncations and rhyming patterns. On page 28 (right), London continues with more scansions and rhyming patterns for verses (line) in typical stanzas, containing large numbers of metric feet. It is unclear whether these were taken from *Orthometry* by Brewer.

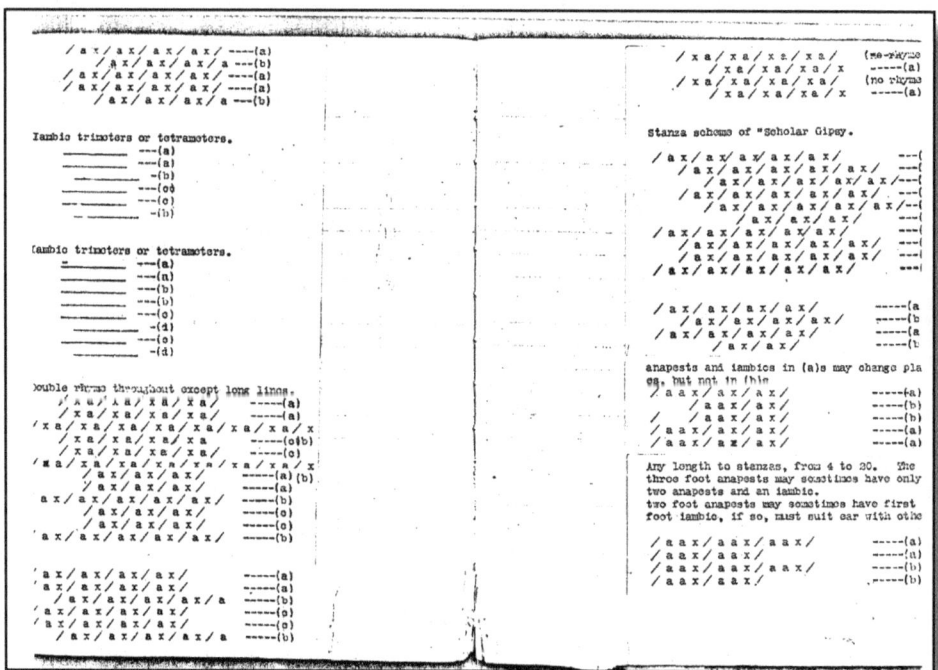

Page 29 & 30: In these two pages London continues his scansions and note taking with more variations of mixed metric feet, anapests and iambics, and rhyming patterns explaining various exceptions. It is unclear whether these were taken from *Orthometry* by Brewer.

APPENDIX B

JACK LONDON:

A CHRONOLOGICAL BIOGRAPHY

1876   Born John Griffith Chaney, at 615 Third Street, San Francisco, California. Son of Flora Wellman (born Massillon, Ohio, August 17, 1843) and William Henry Chaney (born near present-day Chesterville, Maine, January 13, 1821). Chaney, an itinerant astrologer, lived with Flora Wellman during 1874-1875. Chaney deserted his common-law wife upon learning of her pregnancy and later (1897) denied to London that he could have been his father. On September 7, Flora (who used the name Chaney) marries John London, a native of Pennsylvania and Union Army veteran, a widower with two daughters. John London accepts Flora's son as his own and he is named John Griffith London, the middle name deriving from a favorite nephew of Flora Wellman's, Griffith Everhard.

1891   Completes grammar school. Works in a cannery.

1892   Purchases the sloop Razzle-Dazzle with $300 borrowed from his former wet nurse, Daphne Virginia ("Mammy Jenny") Prentiss and becomes "Prince of the Oyster Pirates" on San Francisco Bay. Serves as officer in the Fish Patrol on San Francisco Bay.

1893   Serves several months aboard the sealing schooner Sophia Sutherland in Bering Sea sealing waters and the North Pacific. Returns in summer and on November 12, wins first prize in the San Francisco Call's "Best Descriptive Article" contest for "Story of a Typhoon Off the Coast of Japan."

1894   Joins the western detachment of "Coxey's Army,"—"Kelly's Army"—to march to Washington, D.C. Leaves the ragtag "army" in the Midwest and rides the rails eastward. Is arrested for vagrancy in Niagara Falls, N.Y. in June and serves one month in the Erie County Penitentiary. These experiences he will later chronicle in *The Road* (1907).

1895   Finishes public school education at Oakland High School where he writes sketches and stories for the student magazine *The High School Aegis*.

1896   Joins Socialist Labor Party. Passes entrance examinations and attends the University of California at Berkeley for one semester. Begins seriously studying and writing poetry.

1897   Worked in a laundry before leaving for Alaska in July for the Klondike gold rush and spends the winter in the Yukon. John London dies in Oakland on October 14.

1898   Returns to Oakland in July from Alaska via 2,000 mile boat trip down the Yukon River. Starts log-book called "No 1—MAGAZINE SALES—1898 to May 1900."

Submitted "A Thousand Deaths" to *The Black Cat magazine*, which published the story in May, 1899. The "first money I ever received for a story."

1899 Stops writing poetry and begins writing prose for a living. Publishes first "professional" story, "To the Man on the Trail" in The *Overland Monthly*. December 21, signs contract with Houghton, Mifflin & Co., for a book of short stories.

1900 "An Odyssey of the North" is published in *The Atlantic Monthly*. Marries Bessie Maddern on April 7; on the same day, his first published book, ***The Son of the Wolf*** (1), a collection of Northland fiction, appears.

1901 First daughter, Joan, is born on January 15. ***The God of His Fathers*** (2) is published.

1902 Travels to London, England, where he lives six weeks in the city's East End ghetto, and there gathers material for his brilliant sociological study, ***The People of the Abyss*** (8) (a phrase credited to H. G. Wells.) Second daughter, Bess, is born on October 20. ***Children of the Frost*** (3) and ***The Cruise of the Dazzler*** (4) is published. ***A Daughter of the Snows*** (5), is published by Lippincott's.

1903 William Henry Chaney dies on January 8. ***The Kempton-Wace Letters*** (6), an epistolary exchange with co-author Anna Strunsky on the subject of love, is published by The Macmillan Co. Separates from Bessie London. ***The Call of the Wild*** (7) is published, an instantaneous success. ***The People of the Abyss*** (8) published.

1904 Sails for Japan and Korea as war correspondent for the Hearst Syndicate in the Russo-Japanese War. ***The Faith of Men*** (9) and ***The Sea-Wolf*** (10) are published, London's second most famous novel.

1905 Divorces Bessie Maddern London. Marries Charmian Kittredge on November 20 in Chicago. Purchased his first 129 of the eventual 1400 acres of the Beauty Ranch in Glen Ellen in the Sonoma Valley. Lectures in Midwest and East. ***War of the Classes*** (11), ***The Game*** (12) and ***The Tales of the Fish Patrol*** (13) are published.

1906 Lectures at Yale in January on "The Coming Crisis." Reports on the San Francisco earthquake and fire, April 18, for Colliers. Begins building the *Snark* (named after Lewis Carroll's creation), to sail around the world. ***Moon Face*** (14), ***White Fang*** (15), written as a companion volume to *The Call of the Wild*, and ***Scorn of Women*** (16) are published.

1907 Sails April 23 from San Francisco in *Snark*, visiting Hawaii—including the leper colony at Molokai—the Marquesas Islands, and Tahiti. ***Before Adam*** (17), ***Love of Life*** (18) and ***The Road*** (19) are published.

1908 Returns to California aboard the Mariposa to straighten out financial affairs. Continues *Snark* voyage to Samoa, Fiji Islands, New Hebrides, Solomon Islands, and Australia. ***The Iron Heel*** (20) is published.

Appendix B: A Chronological Biography

1909   Is hospitalized in Sydney, Australia, with a series of tropical ailments. Abandons *Snark* voyage and returns to California on the Scotch collier *Tymeric* via Pitcairn Island, Ecuador, Panama, New Orleans and Arizona. Arrives at Wake Robin Lodge on July 24. ***Martin Eden*** (21), a semi-autobiographical novel, is published.

1910   Step-sister Eliza London Shepard became ranch superintendent. Devotes energies, and funds, to building up his "Beauty Ranch." Wolf House, London's baronial mansion, as construction begins. Birth on June 19, and death on June 21 of the Londons' first child, a daughter named Joy. ***Lost Face*** (22), ***Revolution and Other Essays*** (23), ***Burning Daylight*** (24) and ***Theft*** (25) are published.

1911   With his wife and valet Yoshimatsu Makata, spends summer driving a four-horse carriage through northern California and Oregon and back. ***When God laughs*** (26), ***Adventure*** (27), ***The Cruise of the Snark*** (28) and ***South Sea Tales*** (29) are published.

1912   Sails on March 2 from Baltimore around Cape Horn to Seattle aboard the four-masted barque *Dirigo*, a 148-day voyage. The Londons' second baby lost in miscarriage. ***The house of Pride*** (30), ***A Son of the Sun*** (31) and ***Smoke Bellew*** (32) are published.

1913   Wolf House, on August 22 is mysteriously destroyed by fire, a $70,000 loss, probably caused by spontaneous combustion from oil-soaked rags. Attended San Francisco premier of *The Sea Wolf*, the first feature-length film produced in the U.S. ***The Night Born*** (33) and ***The Abysmal Brute*** (34) published. ***John Barleycorn*** (35), semi-autobiographical novel-treatise on alcoholism, is published. ***The Valley of the Moon*** (36) is also published.

1914   Becomes correspondent for Colliers, at $1100 a week, in Mexican Revolution. Left for Hawaii. ***The Strength of the Strong*** (37) and ***The Mutiny of the Elsinore*** (38) published.

1915   Returns to Hawaii, staying for several months, this time for health reasons. Is warned by doctors of his excessive drinking and poor diet. ***The Scarlet Plague*** (39) and his last great work, ***The Star Rover*** (40), are published.

1916   Resigns from Socialist Party "because of its lack of fire and fight, and its loss of emphasis on the class struggle." ***The Acorn Planter*** (41), ***The Little Lady of the Big House*** (42), and ***The Turtles of Tasman*** (43) are published.

Jack London dies at 7:45 p.m., November 22, of gastrointestinal uremic poisoning.

1917   ***The Human Drift*** (44), ***Jerry of the Islands*** (45) and ***Michael Brother of Jerry*** *(46)* are published.

1918   ***The Red One*** (47) and ***Hearts of Three*** (48) are published.

1919   ***On the Makaloa Mat*** (49) published.

1922	Flora Wellman London (mother) dies on January 4. ***Dutch Courage*** (50) published.
1947	Bessie Maddern London (first wife) dies on September 7.
1955	Charmian Kittredge London (second wife) dies on January 13.
1962	***The Assassination Bureau Ltd*** (51) published.
1971	Joan London (daughter) dies on January 18.
1992	Bess (Becky) London (daughter) dies on March 26.

The grave of Jack London

APPENDIX C

JACK LONDON:

PUBLISHED BOOKS

1	*The Son of the Wolf*	Boston: Houghton Mifflin,	1900
2	*The God of His Fathers & Other Stories*	New York: McClure, Phillips and Co.,	1901
3	*Children of the Frost*	New York: The Macmillan Co.,	1902
4	*The Cruise of the Dazzler*	New York: The Century Co.,	1902
5	*A Daughter of the Snows*	New York: J. B. Lippincott,	1902
6	*The Kempton-Wace Letters*	New York: The Macmillan Co.,	1903
7	*The Call of the Wild*	New York: The Macmillan Co.,	1903
8	*The People of the Abyss*	New York: The Macmillan Co.,	1903
9	*The Faith of Men & Other Stories*	New York: The Macmillan Co.,	1904
10	*The Sea-Wolf*	New York: The Macmillan Co.,	1904
11	*War of the Classes*	New York: The Macmillan Co.,	1905
12	*The Game*	New York: The Macmillan Co.,	1905
13	*Tales of the Fish Patrol*	New York: The Macmillan Co.,	1905
14	*Moon-Face & Other Stories*	New York: The Macmillan Co.,	1906
15	*White Fang*	New York: The Macmillan Co.,	1906
16	*Scorn of Women*	New York: The Macmillan Co.,	1906
17	*Before Adam*	New York: The Macmillan Co.,	1907
18	*Love of Life & Other Stories*	New York: The Macmillan Co.,	1907
19	*The Road*	New York: The Macmillan Co.,	1907
20	*The Iron Heel*	New York: The Macmillan Co.,	1908
21	*Martin Eden*	New York: The Macmillan Co.,	1909
22	*Lost Face*	New York: The Macmillan Co.,	1910
23	*Revolution and Other Essays*	New York: The Macmillan Co.,	1910
24	*Burning Daylight*	New York: The Macmillan Co.,	1910
25	*Theft*	New York: The Macmillan Co.,	1910
26	*When God Laughs & Other Stories*	New York: The Macmillan Co.,	1911
27	*Adventure* *[1]	London: Thomas Nelson & Sons,	1911
28	*The Cruise of the Snark*	New York: The Macmillan Co.,	1911
29	*South Sea Tales*	New York: The Macmillan Co.,	1911
30	*The House of Pride & Other Tales of Hawaii*	New York: The Macmillan Co.,	1912
31	*A Son of the Sun*	New York: Doubleday, Page & Co.,	1912
32	*Smoke Bellew*	New York: The Century Co.,	1912
33	*The Night Born*	New York: The Century Co.,	1913
34	*The Abysmal Brute*	New York: The Century Co.,	1913
35	*John Barleycorn*	New York: The Century Co.,	1913
36	*The Valley of the Moon*	New York: The Macmillan Co.,	1913
37	*The Strength of the Strong*	New York: The Macmillan Co.,	1914
38	*The Mutiny of the Elsinore*	New York: The Macmillan Co.,	1914
39	*The Scarlet Plague*	New York: The Macmillan Co.,	1915
40	*The Jacket* *[2]	London: Mills & Boon Ltd.,	1915

41	*The Acorn Planter*	New York: The Macmillan Co.,	1916
42	*The Little Lady of the Big House*	New York: The Macmillan Co.,	1916
43	*The Turtles of Tasman*	New York: The Macmillan Co.,	1916
44	*The Human Drift*	New York: The Macmillan Co.,	1917
45	*Jerry of the Islands*	New York: The Macmillan Co.,	1917
46	*Michael, Brother of Jerry*	New York: The Macmillan Co.,	1917
47	*The Red One*	New York: The Macmillan Co.,	1918
48	*Hearts of Three*[3]	London: Mills and Boon Ltd.,	1918
49	*On the Makaloa Mat*	New York: The Macmillan Co.,	1919
50	*Dutch Courage & Other Stories*	New York: The Macmillan Co.,	1922
51	*The Assassination Bureau Ltd*	New York: McGraw-Hill Books,	1963

The later published four books are collections of London's previously uncollected or unpublished articles, essays or poetry, which are not contained in any of the earlier books.:

52	*Jack London Reports*	New York: Doubleday and Company	1970
53	*Jack London No Mentor But Myself*	Port Washington, NY: Kennikat Press	1979
54	*Jack London The Unpublished and Uncollected Articles and Essays*	Bloomington, IN: AuthorHouse	2007
55	*The Complete Poetry of Jack London*	New London, CT: Little Red Tree Publishing	2007

Notes:

[1] American edition published later by The Macmillan Co.
[2] American edition retitled **The Star Rover** published later by The Macmillan Co.
[3] American edition published later by The Macmillan Co.

Jack London in his office.

INDEX OF JACK LONDON POEM TITLES AND FIRST VERSES

Poem titles are in bold. First verses are in italics.

Abalone Song	19
The Acorn Planter *(Section E)*	132
A Heart	57
Ah! my brothers, we are mortals,	6
A little sea sprite,	14
A lonely dwelling in a garden bowered,	57
And Some Night	66
"And some night,	66
And the clock went, tick, tick, tick,	24
A Passionate Author To His Love	18
A Trumpet call, a bursting of the sod,	13
Ballade of the False Lover	48
Beautiful Homeland, my own dear Homeland,	65
Be still !	184
Billy met a girlie, he learned to love her so,	25
By Jove! It's George — this is a joy!	49
Cupid's Deal	41
Come write to me and be my Love,	18
Daybreak	4
Effusion	2
Gathered round our standards, boys, we face the fray again;	45
George Sterling	64
Gold	28
Grim prompter of forgotten lines	63
Heaven bless you, my friend—	5
He asked me there to be his bride,	48
He Chortled With Glee	8
He chortled with glee	8
He heard the wondrous tale and went	37
He Never Tried Again	37
His Trip to Hades	56
Homeland (39)	65
Hors De Saison	35
I am your Adam, you are my Eve,	22
If I Were God	10
If I were God one hour	10
I live in hope from day to day,	30
I love to feel the wind's great power	31

In a Year	**18**
In a year, in a year, when the grapes are ripe,	*18*
In slumbers of midnight the Klondyker lay;	*38*
I saw a man open an iris petal	*64*
Je Vis En Espoir	**30**
Just over the way where the rainbow fell,	*55*
Lovers Liturgy	**6**
Man primeval hurled a rock,	*11*
Memory	**63**
"Me tell your fortune? Nay' " she cried;	*41*
Moods	**40**
My Confession	**31**
My Little Palmist	**46**
"Name me the gift of God!"	*61*
Nothing but comes too late with me,	*35*
O Fathers of the Nation,	*43*
Of Man of the Future	**21**
Of man of the future! Who is able to describe him?	*21*
Oh, some folks boast of quail on toast	*19*
Oh You Everybody's Girl	**25**
On the Face of the Earth You Are the One	**22**
Rainbows End	**55**
Red Cloud is late.	*133*
Republican Battle-Hymn	**43**
Republican Rallying Song	**45**
Return of Ulysses — A Modern Version	**49**
Sea Sprite and the Shooting Star	**14**
Sonnet (10)	**13**
Strange was the alchemy through which you passed,	*28*
The blushing dawn the easy illumes,	*4*
The First Poet (Section F)	**184**
The Gift of God	**61**
The Klondyker's Dream	**38**
The leaves stirred softly overhead,	*46*
The Mammon Worshippers	**3**
The room was narrow and cold and grim;	*32*
The Socialist Dream	**32**
The Song of the Flames	**60**
The Way of War	**11**
The Worker and the Tramp	**5**
Thou canst not weep;	*2*
Tick! Tick! Tick!	**24**

Index of Poem Titles and First Verse

Too Late	**68**
Too late' Even Is death too late'	*68*
Trying to miss his trip to Hades,	*56*
We are motes of sunshine stolen	*60*
We worshipped at alien altars; we bowed our heads in the dust;	*3*
When He Came In	**9**
When he came in	*9*
When All the World Shouted My Name	**69**
When all the world shouted my name,	*69*
Who has not laughed with the skylark,	*40*
Your Kiss	**67**
Your kiss, beloved, was to me	*67*

INDEX OF POETS AND AUTHORS

Abbott, Eleanor Hallowell	97
Addison, Joseph	221
Alighieri, Dante	77
Appenzeller, H.G.	113
Applegarth, Edward	xviii, 4, 29, 30, 34, 36
Applegarth, Mabel	xxi, 29
Ashe, Thomas	80, 83
Austin, Alfred	93
Aytoun, William Edmonstoune	223
Banks, Elizabeth	108
Barclay, Alexander	104
Baring-Gould, Sabine	222
Beadle, J. H.	110(2)
Bierce, Ambrose	xxiii, 20
Bingham, Hiram	118
Blake, William	118
Blair, Eric (see: George Orwell)	viii
Bland, Edith Nesbit	94
Bland, James A.	108
Blatchford, Robert	84
Blind, Mathlide	85
Bonar, Horatius	105
Buckley, R. Bishop	108
Burns, Robert	xvi, 222
Brandt, Sebastian	104
Brewer, Robert F.	xvi, 219, 220, 221, 222, 223, 224, 225, 226
Browning, Robert	xviii, xxi, 76, 78(2), 79
Browning, Elizabeth Barrett	89
Byron, George Gordon (Lord Bryon),	75(3). 224
Carroll, Lewis	228
Campbell, Joseph (see: Seosamh MacCathmhaoil)	107
Carman, William Bliss	106
Chaucer, Geoffrey	xix
Cheney, John Vance	87
Connor, J. Torrey	xxiii
Coolbrith, Ina	xv
Cowper, William	223
Davis, Thomas Osborne	92
Day, Thomas Fleming	89
Dobson, Henry Austin	224
Dowson, Ernest	90
Dryden, John	xvi, xxiii, 29, 221, 222, 224
Elliot, Charles Samuel	124
Emerson, Ralph	79

Index of Poets and Authors

Finch, Lucine	118
FitzGerald, Edward	xxiii, 88, 102, 103, 112
Furth, Seymour	120
Garland, Hamlin Hannibal	91
Garnett, Richard	77
Gilmore, Patrick Sarsfield (aka: Louis Lambert)	
Goldsmith, Oliver	83
Gutmanis, June	121
Grant, John Cameron	225
Harben, Will Nathaniel	110
Heben, George	113
Heelan, Will A.	120
Henley, William Ernest	xxiii, 78, 100, 101, 103, 104
Herrick, Robert	221
Hopper, James (Jimmy)	iv
Hovey, Richard	106
Hulbert, Homer Bezaleel	113, 114
Irwin, Wallace	xxii
Johnson, Samuel (Johnsoned)	29
Johnson, Robert	75
Jones, George Heber	113
Kemp, Harry	107
Kipling, Rudyard	75, 76, 81, 84, 87, 88, 94(2), 102(2), 105, 112, 115, 116, 117, 126, 203
Khayyám, Omar	81, 88, 102, 103, 198, 199, 200
Knight, Joseph Philip	74
Kubanoff, Hassack	23, 24
Laing, Andrew	200
Lambert, Louis (see Gilmore)	76
Lanier, Sidney	81(2)
Le Gallienne, Richard	xxiii, 102(2), 112, 198
Lewis, Alfred Henry	91
Lili'uokalani,	98(3), 120
London, Charmian	iv, vii, xiii, xxiii(3), 197(2), 198(5), 199(4), 200(2), 201(6), 207, 228, 230
Longfellow, Henry Wadsworth	xviii, 74, 78, 86, 131, 221
Lowell, James Russell	80, 101
MacCathmhaoil, Seosamh (aka: Joseph Campbell)	107
Marlowe, Christopher	18
Matthews, Brander	224
Milton, John	82, 90
Moore, Michael	222
Moran, E. P.	120
Moret, Neil	65
Morris, William	85, 200

Neihardt, John Gueisenau	99, 205
Noyes, Henry	xxii
O'Hara, John Myers	79
Ohlinger, F.	113
Outram, George	220
Orwell. George	viii
Page, Curtis Hidden	93
Parry, Joseph	109
Patten, William	116
Percy, Thomas	xxiii
Petrarca, Francesco	77
Poe, Edgar Alan	223
Pope, Alexander	xvi, 221
Powers, Stephen	116
Pratt, C. Charles	16
Riseman, Joseph	23, 24, 25
Roberts, Charles G.D.	225
Rosetti	xxiii
Scollard, Clifford	225
Scott, Duncan Campbell	99
Shackleton, Ernest, (Sir)	104
Shakespeare, William	xvi, xviii, 87, 102, 222
Shapiro, Maurice	120
Shay, Frank	90
Spencer, Edmund (Spenserian)	xvi, 29
Shelley, Percy Bysshe	xvi, 222
Sterling, George	iv, vii(2), xxii, xxiii, xxiv, 20,(2) 64(4), 105, 106, 119(2), 183(3), 239
Stevenson, Burton Egbert	94
Stewart, George H.	100
Stoddard, Charles Warren	100, 101
Stone, Irving	1
Strunsky, Anna	x, xxii, xxii(2), xxiv, 18, 199, 223, 228
Swinburne, Algernon Charles	xix, xxi, xxiii 82, 89, 92, 100
Symons, Arthur Williams	xxiii, 88, 111
Thomson, James	106
Thompson, Francis	29
Tennyson, Alfred Lord	xvi, xx, xxi, 85, 95, 222, 223
Wallace, Irvin	xxii
Wesley, Charles	109
Westervelt, William Drake	120, 121, 122
White, Charles Albert	109
Wilde, Oscar	95
Willard, Emma Hart	74
Wordsworth, William	77(2), 112, 113
Wycombe, W. de	113

BIBLIOGRAPHY OF JACK LONDON'S POETRY

"Abalone Song," *Valley of the Moon*, The Macmillan Co. Co., (New York), (October 1913), pages 386-387 also pages 391-392.

"And Some Night," *The Complete Poetry of Jack London*, Little Red Tree Publishing (New London, CT), (December 2007).

"A Passionate Author to His Love," *Recreation*, (September 1904).

"Ballade of the False Lover," *The Complete Poetry of Jack London*, Little Red Tree Publishing (New London, CT), (December 2007).

"Cupid's Deal," *The Complete Poetry of Jack London*, Little Red Tree Publishing (New London, CT), (December 2007).

"Daybreak," *National Magazine* (Boston) XIV, 5 (August 1901), page 547.

"Effusion," "The Human Drift," *The Forum*, (New York), (January 1911)

"Future Wars" (written in June 1899, no extant copy)

"George Sterling," *The Complete Poetry of Jack London*, Little Red Tree Publishing (New London, CT), (December 2007).

"The Gift of God," *The Complete Poetry of Jack London*, Little Red Tree Publishing (New London, CT), (December 2007).

"Gold," *The Complete Poetry of Jack London*, Little Red Tree Publishing (New London, CT), (December 2007).

"A Heart," *The Complete Poetry of Jack London*, Little Red Tree Publishing (New London, CT), (December 2007).

"He Chortled With Glee," *Town Topics* (New York), XLI, 16 (April 20, 1899), page 8.

"He Never Tried Again," *The Complete Poetry of Jack London*, Little Red Tree Publishing (New London, CT), (December 2007).

"His Trip to Hades," *The Complete Poetry of Jack London*, Little Red Tree Publishing (New London, CT), (December 2007).

"Homeland," *The Complete Poetry of Jack London*, Little Red Tree Publishing (New London, CT), (December 2007).

"Hors de Saison," *The Complete Poetry of Jack London*, Little Red Tree Publishing (New London, CT), (December 2007).

"If I Were God," *Town Topics* (New York), XLI, 19 (May 11, 1899), page 18.

"In a Year," *California Birthday Book*, Arroyo Guild Press, (Los Angeles), (January 1901)., page 342.

"Je Vis En Espoir," *The Complete Poetry of Jack London*, Little Red Tree Publishing (New London, CT), (December 2007).

"The Klondyker's Dream," *The Complete Poetry of Jack London*, Little Red Tree Publishing (New London, CT), (December 2007).

"The Lover's Liturgy," *The Raven* (Oakland) II, 1 (February 1901), page 1.

"Mammon Worshippers," *Saturday Evening Post*, (New York), (December 25, 1976).

"Memory," *The Complete Poetry of Jack London*, Little Red Tree Publishing (New London, CT), (December 2007).

"Moods," *The Complete Poetry of Jack London*, Little Red Tree Publishing (New London, CT), (December 2007).

"My Confession," *The Complete Poetry of Jack London*, Little Red Tree Publishing (New London, CT), (December 2007).

"My Gentle Nurse," (written in June 1898, no extant copy).

"My Little Palmist," *The Complete Poetry of Jack London*, Little Red Tree Publishing (New London, CT), (December 2007).

"Of Man of the Future," *In the Footsteps of Jack London*, Komsomol Pravda, (Moscow), (Sept. 20 and 23, 1959).

"Oh You Everybody's Girl," Melodius Music Co., (Boston), (1915).

"On the Face of the Earth You Are the One," Melodius Music Co., (Boston), (1915).

"Rainbow's End," *The Complete Poetry of Jack London*, Little Red Tree Publishing (New London, CT), (December 2007).

"Republican Battle-Hymn," *The Complete Poetry of Jack London*, Little Red Tree Publishing (New London, CT), (December 2007).

"Republican Rallying Song," *The Complete Poetry of Jack London*, Little Red Tree Publishing (New London, CT), (December 2007).

"The Return of Ulysses – a Modern Version," *The Complete Poetry of Jack London*, Little Red Tree Publishing (New London, CT), (December 2007).

"Rich Morsels," (written in March 1899, no extant copy).

"The Sea Sprite and the Shooting Star," Keesling Press (Campbell, CA), (1932).

"The Socialist Dream," *The Complete Poetry of Jack London*, Little Red Tree Publishing (New London, CT), (December 2007).

"The Song of the Flames," *The Complete Poetry of Jack London*, Little Red Tree Publishing (New London, CT), (December 2007).

"Sonnet," *Dilettante* (Alameda, Ca) VII, 8 (February 1901), page 169.

"Still Hunt," (written in November 1898, no extant copy).

"Thlinket Anger," (written in March 1899, no extant copy).

"Tick! Tick! Tick!," Melodius Music Co., (Boston), (1915).

"Too Late," *The Complete Poetry of Jack London*, Little Red Tree Publishing (New London, CT), (December 2007).

"The Way of War," *Once a Week* (Oakland) California Edition, 2 (Oct. 27, 1906).

"When All the World Shouted My Name," *The Complete Poetry of Jack London*, Little Red Tree Publishing (New London, CT), (December 2007).

"When He Came In," *Town Topics* (New York) XLI, 19 (April 26, 1899), page 23.

"The Worker and the Tramp," *The Comrade* (New York) I, 4 (January 1902), page 13.

"Your Kiss," *The Complete Poetry of Jack London*, Little Red Tree Publishing (New London, CT), (December 2007).

ABOUT THE AUTHOR

DANIEL J. WICHLAN

Daniel J. Wichlan was born and raised in St. Louis, Missouri where he attended elementary school and high school. He was the sixth of seven children and his father, who was an avid reader, gave Dan the gift of reading in the form of a library card and a collection of Jack London short stories for his tenth birthday. After completing high school, Dan gained a degree in Industrial Engineering from St. Louis University and was awarded a teaching assistantship to Kansas State University where he gained a Masters in Industrial Engineering. He subsequently declined a Ph.D. teaching fellowship to Purdue University in favor of embarking on a professional career in financial services.

After beginning a career in the financial services industry in St. Louis, he relocated to San Francisco where he was an IT systems executive with both Bank of America and Charles Schwab & Company, from where he left in 1991 and helped to found and manage three different Internet related companies. He retired from the information systems profession in 1999.

A life long independent London scholar, of legendary status, Dan has spent much of his discretionary time over the last 30 years collecting material for this and other books related to Jack London. He is the editor of *Jack London: The Unpublished and Uncollected Articles and Essays*. He is also a contributor to the forthcoming Oxford University Press *Handbook of Jack London*. Dan is a member of the Jack London Foundation for which he is a frequent banquet speaker and a board member of the Jack London Society. He has given numerous papers on both London's fiction and nonfiction at the Jack London Symposiums and the Popular Culture Association conferences. He received the 2005 Jack London Foundation "Man of the Year" Award, and Dan's research at The Huntington Library was sponsored by Earle Labor, the country's leading London scholar. Dan's work is referenced in Earl's definitive biography *Jack London An American Life*.

www.ingramcontent.com/pod-product-compliance
Lightning Source LLC
Chambersburg PA
CBHW080457110426
42742CB00017B/2920